Errata
WORLD COLORS

The following are corrections for typographical errors.

Page 6 — "...we will come to find regional costume dolls as [one] of the most accurate..."

Page 33 — "Samso bride, left; married lady, right." *should read* "North Falster bride, left; Samso bride, right."

Page 36 — "(Left to right): Kirkkonummi; Finland; (male) Munsala" *should read* "(Left to right): Munsala; Finland (male); Kirkkonummi"

Page 65 — "Philadel-phia" *should read* "Philadelphia"; "Szere-lemhegyi" *should read* "Szerelemhegyi"

Page 95 — "Michoácan" *should read* "Michoacán"

Page 111 — "LA MONTUNO" *should read* "LA MONTUNA"

Page 123 — *This should be added:* "*Please note that the Romanian textiles shown here are, as noted, from the Transylvania area. The Oltenia region is not however part of the Transylvania area."

Page 125 — "MEXICO" *should read* "RUSSIA"; "Vyshnyaya Zalegoslich village,..." *should read* "Vyshnyaya Zalegoshch village,..."

Page 127 — "The dolls were imported [in]to Russia and costumed..."

WORLD COLORS

DOLLS
&
DRESS

by Susan Hedrick
&
Vilma Matchette

FOLK &
ETHNIC
DOLLS

Photography by
CHARLES BACKUS

Published by

Hobby
House
Press™

Hobby House Press, Inc.
Grantsville, Maryland 21536

DEDICATIONS

This book is dedicated to
Jordan Cole and René Matchette by Vilma Matchette, and
to the loving memory of Roy D. Pickel by his daughter Susan Hedrick.

ACKNOWLEDGEMENTS

Without the help and support of many people who went the extra mile (or two!), this book simply would not have come about.

Many of the dolls in this book reside at the Rosalie Whyel Museum of Doll Art in Bellevue, Washington (where I am Curator). Rosalie has supported this book from its very beginnings, and tolerated my many book-related "distractions." She generously and gladly lent her wonderful dolls, who add immeasurably to the scope of this book and the beauty of its pages.

Jane Gregory and her daughter Sarah will find many of their dolls here; their extensive, well-documented collection was a joy to work with. Recently, the Gregorys munificently gifted much of this collection to the Rosalie Whyel Museum of Doll Art. Pat Foster's fabulous collection of antique dolls in regional dress was always available to us. Jaye Delbridge, Gail Hiatt, Diana Honda, Jim and Bea McDonald, Noreen Ott and Mindi Reid willingly lent their dolls to be photographed.

I appreciate the faith that Gary Ruddell of Hobby House Press has shown in this project. He listened to my arguments for a mostly color and susequently more expensive book on a subject that is just beginning to catch on again amongst collectors.

Photographer Charles Backus's patience and sense of humor with these sometimes uncooperative dolls and their horrible ("gotta hide 'em") stands is pretty amazing.

Numerous people have aided our project by discovering research materials and sharing their knowledge: Clara Abinanti, Maria Argyriadi, Harriett Beerfas, Dorothy and Jane Coleman, Marjory Fainges, Erika Gärdtner of Camillo Gärdtner & Co. (Baitz Dolls), Margaret Groninger, Lorna Lieberman, Ethelyn McKim, Taime Mok and Eva Moskovsky. Diana Honda and Kim Maloney spent many hours at the computer keyboard. Countless others have contributed in some manner or another to the success of this book. God bless them all!

And finally, I want to send about a million thanks to my husband and friend, Basil Hedrick. Without question he has remained my strongest backer, putting up with every problem caused by (or blamable on) THE BOOK! He is probably as glad as we are to see it finished.

Susan Hedrick

For assistance during the process of writing this book I would like to thank the following: Lloyd Cotsen, Patricia MacDonald, Margaret Hord, Cath Oberholtzer, Jordan Cole, Marge Posner, René Matchette and David Clelland. I would also like to thank the entire staff at the Lynnwood Public Library Reference Department, and all the libraries around the country who graciously loaned invaluable materials.

Vilma Matchette

Front Cover: 35" ceramic head doll, "Anfisa," in the Russian costume of Tula Province. Made by Alexandra Kukinova, Moscow, 1995.
Title Page: 17" French bisque head lady doll dressed in the costume of Attica, Greece, 1880s. *Pat Foster collection.*
Back Cover: 7"-16" English wooden dolls, c.1790-1820, dressed by the Eastern Cree Indians of the Hudson Bay area in what is now Canada. *Rosalie Whyel Museum of Doll Art.*

Additional copies of this book may be purchased at $75.00 (plus postage and handling) from
Hobby House Press, Inc.
1 Corporate Drive
Grantsville, Maryland 21536
1-800-554-1447
or from your favorite bookstore or dealer.

ISBN: 0-87588-473-3

TABLE OF CONTENTS

FOREWORD 3

COUNTRIES *(Listed in Alphabetical order)*: 7-176

BIBLIOGRAPHY

Dolls 177

Costume 180

COSTUME GLOSSARY 186

INDEX 189

FOREWORD

Annie Fields Alden, a doll collector, wrote in the November 1898 issue of *Ladies Home Journal*: "...when my friends...visit foreign countries, I have always said: 'Bring me dolls of the people.' I have found that these dolls reveal more about their countries than one might first suppose...I have expected them to show the differences of costume and of color, but they do much more than this — they show the airs, the spirit, the general trend of thought of the countries which they represent. One might say with a great deal of truth: 'Show me the dolls of a country and I will show you that country'." (Coleman, Dorothy S. and Evelyn Jane, "Poupées du Littoral," *Spinning Wheel*, April 1976)

Annie Fields Alden — perhaps every bit as enthusiastic over and biased towards these dolls as I am — hit upon a truth that is even greater today, almost 100 years later. As costumes and customs that defined regions and countries in years past have declined and even vanished, we must now look at objects like books, postcards, and dolls to recall this past. In this book, we combine each of these elements — the gathered knowledge from books, the illustrations of "picture" postcards, and the dolls — to continue and hopefully advance this understanding of history.

11" (seated) Hungarian pressed cloth doll in costume of the Trans-Danube area, by "Marika" Kovacs, Budapest, 1980s.

How it all started

Working together on an exhibit of folk and regional costume dolls for the Rosalie Whyel Museum of Doll Art, Vilma Matchette and I bemoaned the lack of a good book (in print) on the subject. Even the out-of-print books had their drawbacks: only black and white photos of the most colorful dress in the world, or color photographs that were too small to do the dolls any justice. We decided, on that fateful day nearly five years ago, that if a book was to happen we had to write it!

Since then, several new books have appeared on the dolls; it would appear that this is a subject whose time has finally come. However, our approach was to be different — emphasis was planned to be, and has continued to be on *both* the dolls, including their history and makers, *and* on complete identification of the costumes and their significance.

With this equal emphasis on the dolls and their costumes, we are aiming to appeal to both doll and costume collectors and researchers, plus museums that probably own some of both.

It was to be a good partnership. Vilma's lifelong work on folk costume, and her incredible library of books on the subject, enabled her to take on a daunting task: the whole world! She has identified all of the costumes and fully described them for the book. And my own knowledge of and interest in dolls (of just about any type) let me happily dig into an area that required quite a bit of fascinating primary research. The information and commentary on dolls is my work.

By providing large, professional photographs of the dolls, we can illustrate their incredible variety of color, texture and ornament. We also hope to prove what we (and a devoted group of collectors) have learned: that the dolls are truly wonderful as well as fascinating to collect and learn about. They are an educational tool for more than just children; believe me, I have learned more geography — *enjoyably* — through these dolls in the last five years than I ever did in school.

What to call them?

Russian "Village Boy," one of a series of beautifully-crafted stockinet dolls in regional costume, 1930s.

One of the problems in dealing with this kind of doll is that no one seems to agree on what to call them. "Ethnic," today, refers more to racial or cultural divisions such as Slavic, African-American, Hispanic, or Asian. "Provincial costume" sounds a bit derogatory — a commentary on the sometimes rather parochial areas that the dolls represent. For a while, we were tempted to call them "international" dolls, but that moniker is really awkward (especially for a book title). Personally, I like the term "folk" and use it a lot to describe the costumes, but in doll circles it usually means "primitive."

The Costume Society of America has expended much effort over this same problem of what to call the costumes themselves; they prefer to call them "world costume." So, shall we call them "world dolls"? "National costume dolls" they are most certainly *not,* for there is really no such thing; "regional costume dolls" is a more appropriate label.

Why didn't we include...?

For this book, we tried to present a range of countries; we couldn't begin to adequately cover all, or even most of, the world. People's favorites, or their special interests, are apt to have been left out. For this I apologize, in advance! We were just not able to find interesting and accurately-costumed dolls from everywhere. Perhaps there will be a need for "volume two."

It was crucial to represent the history and evolution of regional dolls by presenting examples from the early 19th century to the present day. We wished to illustrate dolls of many different types of materials: wood, rubber, papier-mâché, china (glazed porcelain), and bisque (unglazed porcelain). Interestingly and significantly, cloth dolls make up our largest majority. Cloth is an inexpensive, readily-available medium that is available to nearly every doll maker.

Some regional costumes are found over and over again on dolls; for instance, Roma in Italy, Berne Canton in Switzerland, Alsace and Brittany in France, Rättvik in Sweden, Volendam in the Netherlands, and others you will discover here. We have emphasized these costumes so you can learn to readily identify them. Other illustrated costumes occur only rarely, but the dolls and the costumes are so extraordinary that they just have to be savored!

From the beginning, our major criteria for choosing dolls were: 1) that they illustrate a costume well (many tourist dolls simply do not) and 2) that the dolls be visually interesting.

It was not important to us (as it is to some collectors and purists) that the doll be made in the country it represents. This would have left out so many of the spectacular antique dolls that really are (and in a few cases are not, which is pointed out) costumed authentically.

We are not including the internationally-costumed dolls by American companies such as Madame Alexander and Effanbee. These dolls are cute and quite collectible, but the costumes are often rather generic.

Despite appearances, there was really not a concentrated effort to present so many of the charming, mainly cloth, dolls offered by Kimport and other importers from the 1930s to the 1960s. These dolls simply continuously fit our above-described criteria. Plus, they are quite readily and inexpensively (with a few major exceptions) available to the collector. Also, these 20th century cloth "foreign dolls" (as Kimport regularly called them) have had very little research or publication done about them. This was an area ripe for delving into!

On becoming addicted to postcards

An essential goal of our book was to show how similar (or dissimilar) the dolls' costumes are to those worn by real people. The idea to use vintage postcards for illustrations was, by turns, both brilliant and addictive. Now I have become a devoted col-

lector of these wonderful old pictures that go so well with the dolls. Besides, what are two things that tourists have collected since the early 1900s? — dolls and postcards.

Regional costume dolls — a checkered history

Once collected by royalty like Queen Victoria and the Queen of Romania, in the past 30 years these dolls have been mostly relegated to boxes under dealer's tables, box lots at auction, and a lumping-together of anything in costume — good, bad or otherwise.

It wasn't always this way with collectors. During the "Kimport Period" (as I call it) of the mid 1930s to the 1950s or '60s, a good-sized group of collectors bought these "modern" regional dolls because they were charming, available and affordable. The concept of "antique" dolls in the 1930s had an entirely different meaning when one could still buy some bisque dolls new or "used." The more "sophisticated" and monied collectors usually bought the older china and parian-head dolls.

World War II destroyed many of Kimport Dolls' best sources. Zygmunt Allina of Poland, for instance, made grand Polish dolls (see our Polish bandit Janosik on page 118) — but the company simply vanished with the fall of Warsaw to Hitler's army. Kimport persisted, continuing what doll lines they could and ferreting out others like "Narodna Radinost," whose exquisite small dolls representing the ethnic groups of (the former) Yugoslavia were a major seller.

A venerable group of female cloth doll makers, some known

and many yet to be discovered, burst onto the doll scene. They created dolls in folk costumes that are every bit the equal in quality and beauty of, for instance, the venerated Lenci dolls. Margit Szerelemhegyi ("Marga") of Hungary, Ronnaug Petterssen of Norway, Baronne Sandra Belling of Syria, and Ingeborg Nielsen of Denmark (the latter two are "rediscovered" in this book) are just a few of the known makers. There are literally hundreds of unknown,

A typical cloth tag from the Kimport Company of Independence, Missouri. Kimport brought quality regional dolls to American collectors, 1930s-1970s.

or little-known, makers that still deserve attention.

This renaissance of cloth doll makers, continuing the tradition of cloth as a "woman's medium," follows in a long line of seminal names, from Izannah Walker to Martha Chase, and Käthe Kruse to Madame Scavini ("Lenci").

More and more will be heard about these talented makers of regional dolls in days to come, as we begin to recognize and appreciate their art.

As interest in modern "play" dolls like *Barbie®* and *Ginny* took off in the 1960s and '70s — a nostalgia-based collecting that has not yet begun to hit its peak — collecting of modern folk costume dolls dropped off. More collectors took an avid interest in antique dolls, especially the bisque ones, and became very knowledgeable. The further that we have come from the days that these costumes were worn on a daily basis, the less we understand or recognize the dolls that wear them (although they seem no less complicated to me than the hundreds of Barbie® outfits and accessories!).

And their future...

With the increase in prices for all of the above dolls from bisque to Barbie®, comes a greater sophistication and a demand for originality. No longer do we want a French lady doll redressed in rayon or polyester. We want the original clothes when possible, which often means a regional costume. Antique dolls in folk costume are beginning to be not only appreciated, but quite desirable (if auction prices are any indicator).

Collectors of German character dolls — many of which were dressed in regional costume because of this movement's emphasis on real or "natural" children (more on this in the book) — are snapping up these dolls in folk dress and paying quite high prices. An exhibit of character dolls at a national conference of doll collectors featured many of these treasured dolls in original (and quite authentic) regional dress.

Many of the dolls shown in this book, especially the "Kimport period" ones that I spoke of before, are one of the real "sleepers" of the doll collecting world, and well worth collecting before they, too, go up in value and everyone catches on.

What do they mean to us now, these dolls in costumes forever vanished, other than for festivals or folk dancers? Do they have any further educational value?

Just as we search costume and ladies' books to understand the history of dress and social customs of the "western" world, we will come to find regional costume dolls as of the most accurate and remarkable documents of how the "rest of the world" lived.

For instance, the Eastern Cree male doll seen in these pages has proven to be one of the only surviving depictions of male Cree dress of the late 18th-early 19th century. His significance to that culture and the people who study it is immeasurable.

What can you gain from the book?

I hope that this book will help you to recognize and identify your regional dolls. And to be interested in further research, using our bibliography to help, about the costumes we did not have room to show. But, most of all, I hope that this volume will help you appreciate both the marvelous dolls and their vibrant, wondrous costumes.

So, perhaps Annie Fields Alden, the doll collector we met at the first of my story, really did glimpse a major truth — that the dolls of a country are one of its finest visual records.

Susan Hedrick
Bellevue, Washington
January 1996

A Costume Note:

We can no longer use vague terminology to discuss dolls in "provincial," "ethnic," or "foreign" costume. Doll scholarship, in general, has moved forward in recent times, especially in terms of historical and technical aspects. Work on the subject of dolls in folk dress has not advanced to the same degree.

In this book, we will attempt to designate costumes and makers in a specific manner. In identifying, I plan to particularize each costume by its country, province, region, and town or village if at all possible. I will further attempt to be explicit about the nature of the costumes. Is it festive or work day, ritual, seasonal, that of married or unmarried, young or old?

There does exist in doll costume, a generic style. A good example is the so-called Dutch costume so popular in the '20s, '30s, and beyond, which illustrated some features of the clothes of the Netherlands, but was never intended to represent anything specific.

There are also costumes and dolls described as Oriental although even these contain clues that will distinguish Chinese from Japanese, and perhaps that is the least we can do for this oft maligned classification.

The doll producers have not always been careful about ethnicity, and for legitimate reasons. At various times, it has not been considered important. After all, these were toys created for the market place, and not meant to be examples of cultural veracity.

I have hopes that the depth and complexity of dolls and folk costume will be revealed to the reader in some small way.

Vilma Matchette

Kabul

About the Dolls

This pair of dolls from Afghanistan are fun and kind of funky: the gentleman with "killer eyebrows" under a wrapped turban, and woman with stark white makeup, kohled eyes and brightly rouged cheeks under her "chadri" or veil. Both have flat, gloved hands cut out of leather.

Another group of Afghani dolls arrived as a donation to the Rosalie Whyel Museum too late for this book (hopefully, there will be a volume two). They are small cloth dolls representing a variety of costumes, a gift of the woman who supervised the self-help group who made the dolls.

Still another style of cloth dolls from this country are found: one woman in particular wears a "chemical" green (this color does not exist in nature!) robe. It is intriguing to note all the different dolls from this small country!

Costume Description

She has a loose scarf over her head; a checked tunic; full loose pants. All covered by the enveloping CHADRI (singular) for outdoor wear. Colors, and shirt and tunic lengths may differ, the garments stay the same.

He has a white turban; a long open sleeve shirt covered by a vest and long loose pants.

Female with chadri worn down.

8-1/2"—9" Maker unknown
Kabul, Afghanistan c.1940s-1950s
Cloth head with painted features, black yarn wig, cloth body over wire armature, leather hands
AFGHANISTAN, KABUL (on base)

Woman's tunic, detail of yoke, Afghanistan, late 20th century.

ALBANIA

Shkoder (Scutari)

8-1/4" Near East Industries
Athens, Greece c.1939
Pressed cloth head, hand-painted
features, auburn floss wig, cloth body
with wire-jointed arms, separate thumbs
KIMPORT (cloth tag)
*Courtesy of the Rosalie Whyel Museum
of Doll Art*

The dolls are always charmingly hand-painted with brick-red to rust-red facial colors. Notice that the lips of the male doll are outlined, an extra feature not often found in small dolls made in fairly large numbers. Each doll wears leather or cloth shoes, sewn with tiny hand-stitches.

Costume Description

Urban style dress of Ottoman influence: kerchief with red trim tied around head; white blouse or chemise with open sleeve edged in gold lace; full white pantaloons in cotton or silk; red velvet sleeveless coat bordered in gold; sheer sash with gold embroidery and slippers or mules.

He displays a white felt TARBOOSH or fez, headwear unique to Albania. This is said to have been red before 1881 and afterwards white to distance themselves from the Ottoman form. White linen shirt; a short sleeved jacket of black wool called a GJURDIN (singular). This has wool tufts and wool fringe on a sailor collar. This collar is put over the head when it rains or the jacket slung over the shoulders when it is sunny. A red under-jacket or vest may be worn called a MINTAN (singular). Fringed beige sash which should be tucked in, may also be in dark red; white semi-wide pants named BREKUSHA (singular) and red shoes with blue pompons. A natural colored native sandal would be more usual.

About the Dolls

A winsome little pair of cloth dolls by Near East Industries, a division of the Near East Foundation, an organization founded to help refugees in the Balkans. Another trio of these dolls can be found here under Greece (Lefkas), and dolls were made from countries ranging from Jordan (Palestine) to Montenegro. An early, larger example of Near East Industries' work is photographed under Macedonia.

Kimport dolls brought in many of these delightful dolls during the late 1930s and 1940s, making an exception to their rule that any international dolls they sold had to be actually made in the country they represented. The dolls of the Near East Industries were made in Athens, Greece by Balkan refugees.

ALGERIA

About the Dolls

Dressed as lovely belles of exotic Algeria (North Africa), these composition (and often bisque-head) dolls are nearly always French. A bisque version that was undressed revealed two things: first, the bodies are greatly elongated and crude (the dolls look much better dressed!) and second, the doll's trouser-type skirt was stuffed with a 1912 Algerian newspaper written in French. Algeria was a French possession until 1962.

Costume Description

Best attire: on her head is a pink silk under kerchief with glass ornaments and gold tinsel band; a silk veil over; necklace and pin in Christmas beads; pink brocade tunic, top edged in a tinsel band, lower edge ends in a wide lace flounce; wide Ottoman style silk pants; gold tinsel belt.

55 - La belle Fathma

12" Attributed to S.F.B.J. Paris, France 1930s
Composition socket head, painted blue eyes, brown human hair, five piece papier-mâché body
Not marked
Courtesy of the Rosalie Whyel Museum of Doll Art

Late 19th century urban Algerian woman.

7" Mattaldi Buenos Aires, Argentina c.1940
Wooden head, painted features, black floss hair, crude wooden body, jointed at shoulders and elbows, paper hands
MATTALDI LTDA. // SARMIENTO 667 // B. AIRES (sticker on base)

About the Dolls

The hard-working gaucho, prevalent throughout parts of South America (see another pair from Uruguay, page 172), is romanticized just like the American cowboy. He certainly does cut a dashing and colorful figure. In doll form, he is often paired with a country girl in ruffled print dress and long braids.

A similar gaucho doll is illustrated in the 1939 Kimport catalog, and again in 1941. "Ricardo of Argentina," their romantic description reads, "has probably broken all hearts between Panama and Tierra del Fuego." "Handsome Ricardo" could be acquired by love-struck collectors for only $3.45!

Costume Description

Her hair in braids, tied with headband and red ribbons; orange neckerchief; cotton print dress with deep flounce at lower edge; white cotton apron; plaid cotton petticoat; holding a gourd for MATE (tea).

Gaucho or cowboy: grey felt hat; white shirt; red neckerchief; black sateen short jacket and special draped pants with red border; wide leather belt ornamented by coins and metal chains; white fringed underdrawers; soft natural colored boots, and he carries a rope. His suit will nearly always be dark or somber, the kerchief being his bright accent.

These costumes are seen in Argentina, Uruguay, and parts of Brazil. They are influenced by colonial dress and by the horseman's lifestyle. Her colors and fabric prints will vary but the form will remain the same. The apron may be omitted.

Argentinian couple in dance, c.1930s.

Native Australian

13"—14" Sarah Midgley Sydney, Australia c.1940

Pressed cloth face with painted features, black mohair wig, cloth body with swing-jointed arms and legs, stitched fingers and toes, separate thumbs

REG. 71899 (LOGO) TRADE MARK // "THE SARAH // MIDGLEY // BUDGERREE DOLL" // COPYRIGHT // 11523"

Courtesy of the Rosalie Whyel Museum of Doll Art

About the Dolls

Sarah Baron Midgley was born in England in 1864 and moved as a child to Australia, where she encountered her first Aboriginal people. She and her sister made special friends with two Aboriginal girls, Widgeon and Kummera, who were to inspire Sarah's first dolls many years later.

Sarah married Alfred Midgley in 1886. When his health failed in later years, the resourceful Sarah was left to supplement the family's income. She even started a knitting mill in town. When Alfred died in 1930, Sarah (then in her late 60s) began creating her Aboriginal dolls, and the first ones were named after her childhood friends. Sarah moved to Sydney and took out a registration (patent) for them in 1936.

Her daughter Daisy made the doll's ceramic mask heads. Over this, Sarah stretched a black sateen and painted their captivating faces. The bodies were also made of black sateen and another artist researched and painted the tribal markings on the warriors.

The dolls were sold in shops in Australia; many were brought home by American GIs in World War II. Kimport Dolls imported them to the U.S. in the early 1940s. For more of Sarah Midgley's story, see Marjory Fainges' *Encyclopedia of Australian Dolls*.

Costume Description

Her attire consists of a necklace of seed beads and a loin cloth.

Attached to his head are a group of feathers; white body paint; leather loin cloth; carries a painted bark shield and a wooden spear.

Otztal Valley, Tyrol

About the Doll

The splendid costume of Austria and the lovely French lady doll with an all wooden body are not original to each other. However, the fit is so perfect, and their temporary relationship so harmonious that I could probably tell you otherwise and be completely believable!

I purchased the late 19th century Tyrolean costume separately, and it languished alone in my collection for a while, lacking the perfect doll to model it. After trial and error — coming to the conclusion that this ensemble was definitely made for a lady doll and not a child, I went in search for the "right" one. There she was at my workplace, in the Museum Store of the Rosalie Whyel Museum of Doll Art. I "borrowed" her for the photo shoot; now she must know how a model feels when she has to give those perfect clothes back! And now the costume is back in my collection, alone again (sigh), because I had to give the doll back.

TIROL.   Oetztal.

Austrian Tyrolean couple, late 19th century. She wears the hat and kerchief that our doll is missing.

Costume Description

A conical woolen hat, like the one in the postcard, would have been worn; white cotton gathered blouse, lace ruffle at neck and wrists; pink sateen bodice with red binding and gold braid and lacing; pleated wool skirt in horizontal colored panels — black, blue, and red; gathered blue floral print apron; green, red, and yellow waist ribbon; a black silk kerchief is usually tied around the neck and tucked into the bodice.

Above and opposite page:
14" Maker unknown, possibly Eugene Barrois Paris, France c.1880s
Bisque swivel head on shoulder plate, inset glass eyes, closed mouth, blonde mohair wig, jointed wood body
Not marked

15" François Gaultier Paris, France c.1880
Bisque swivel head on shoulder plate, inset blue glass eyes, blonde mohair wig, kid leather body with gusset jointing
2 (head) 2 F.G. (shoulder plate)
Pat Foster collection

Flanders

About the Doll

Most dolls from Belgium found in the 20th century represent the lace maker, a typical genre dress but not really a folk costume. Belgium "lost" its folk dress very early compared to much of Europe, and subsequently has very little regional costume history, making this splendid François Gaultier doll especially precious.

She is one of the lucky (and now rather scarce) French lady dolls of the latter 19th century who retains her original regional costume. Many of these dolls were later redressed by doll collectors who did not appreciate the regional costumes, feeling that their doll would be "better" and more valuable in a ball gown or similar finery. Today a higher value is placed on originality; now perhaps the dolls will remain, and be understood, in their rare folk dress.

Costume Description

Festive wear: white lace bonnet, blue silk ribbon bow in back; blue earrings and a religious medal on a blue ribbon; black striped cut velvet blouse with white lace collar and cuffs; gathered skirt of striped wool bound in blue cotton; shoulder kerchief and apron of fine printed cotton; white decorative knit stockings and wooden shoes.

Belgium was industrialized rather early which explains the lack of folk dress.

Belgian everyday female dress, early 20th century.

BRAZIL

State of Bahia

18"—19" Maker unknown
Brazil 1930s-1940s

Cloth head with embroidered features, no hair (standing doll), brown human hair (seated doll), cloth body and legs. Cloth over wire arms and separate fingers with attached painted fingernails

Not marked

About the Dolls

I have seen a good number of these dolls in recent years, and it seems that they are inevitably misattributed to the Caribbean. I understand the confusion — they certainly look like and are dressed like what we think of as Caribbean. But we are here to tell you that they are actually dressed as ladies of Bahia, Brazil!

A similar doll in the Rosalie Whyel Museum of Doll Art bears one of those rare and priceless items, an original paper tag. It reads "La F_ranca da Bahia//Barraca Janaina//Mercado Moreli 76." The Museum also has this doll in a Caucasian version.

Elsie Krug, of the Krug International Doll House, sold these dolls through her newsletters; they are described in a long rambling tale of the history of Brazil in her August/September 1943 issue. The dolls came in 11" to 18" sizes and sold for $6.50. Lesley Gordon illustrated one of these dolls ("Caroline of Brazil") in her 1949 book, *A Pageant of Dolls*.

The dolls are really quite appealing, and even humorous in their accuracy down to their attached long fingernails. Our standing doll was purchased from an antique mall in Michigan; her seated companion was purchased in Paris, France!

For costume description refer to page 16.

BRAZIL

State of Bahia

14" João Perotti Manufactura Orbis Sao Paulo, Brazil 1930s-1940s

Pressed felt swivel head with painted features, no ears, black wig, felt body with swing-jointed arms and disc-jointed legs

JOÃO PEROTTI // R.O.J. ALVES LIMITED // SÃO PAULO // INDUSTRIA BRASILEIRA (Paper tag on underclothes)

About the Doll

Several of the workers from the Italian Lenci factory emigrated to South America after World War II. According to Margaret Groninger ("Wee Immigrants: Latin American Dolls," *Doll News*, summer 1986), these workers started a felt doll company called Lencilandia in Argentina, and also possibly the João Perotti firm in São Paulo, Brazil. The Perotti dolls are of a better quality (they are sometimes mistaken for Lenci's work) than the Argentinian company, and also more frequently seen.

Crowned by a basket of fruit — Carmen Miranda-style, this João Perotti girl from Bahia shows the people's love of colorful and festive dress. Bahia, a picturesque town of steep, cobbled streets, was once the capital of Brazil — a 16th century settlement where African slaves, native Brazilians, and Portuguese and Spanish lived.

Costume Description (see pages 15-16)

In general, the girls from Bahia have head kerchiefs topped with baskets of fruit; usually earrings, bracelets, necklaces and rings; white low cut blouses trimmed with lace; rich and colorful skirts. A bright colored scarf may be worn across the body and fastened at the waist, or a vivid sash and sometimes an apron. Cloth shoes with contrasting rosettes and white lace edged petticoats and bright decorated garters are typical.

Prints, colors, flounces all may be different and some garments can be omitted such as the body scarf, the sash and the apron. The costumes of movie star Carmen Miranda were based on this outfit. Katherine Dunham, the well-respected African-American dance anthropologist performed Brazilian dances wearing a version of this ensemble.

Shope people, Sofia District

8"—8-1/2" Maker unknown Bulgaria c.1940

Composition shoulder head, painted features, painted brown hair (Male), brown mohair wig (Female), cloth body with jointed legs, stitched fingers.

Not marked

About the Dolls

The Kimport catalog of 1939 illustrates a 9" Bulgarian doll called "Sergei of Sophia...modeled and painted by a native artist...dressed in finest wools...strictly collection class." "Sergei" sold for $5.75.

These attractive Bulgarian dolls are now rather hard to locate. Our gentleman came first, from one older collection, and then Sarah and Jane Gregory provided the much sought-after lady.

Bulgarian folk dolls for about the last 25 years usually consist of a painted wooden bead for the head, a rudimentary cloth over wire armature body, and a simple costume with painted patterns in lieu of embroidery. Several

people touring the country have been sent with our explicit instructions to search out and buy any quality dolls, and have come back empty-handed.

Costume Description

Young man in festive dress: black fur hat; white shirt embroidered at chest, collar, and open sleeves in red and black; brown jacket embroidered in white around all edges and seams (also seen in blue); red wool sash wrapped several times around the body; white baggy pants with reinforced and decorated knee area; red stockings and primitive sandals. This male doll looks like plate 33 in *Bulgarian National Attire* by Maria Veleva, a well known writer on Bulgarian dress.

Best costume: tied on her head is a pink kerchief with a gold edge. Kerchief would more likely be white. Chemise is of white cotton with open sleeves, embroidered in red and green on chest, sleeve and hem; over this is a dark blue or black sleeveless dress called a SOUKMAN (singular); red stockings and simple native sandals.

274. Costumes bulgares nationales Sofia.
Софийска носия.

Late 19th century man and woman in costumes worn near Sofia, Bulgaria.

Eastern Bulgaria

9" Maker unknown Bulgaria
c.1940
Composition head with painted
features, wooden goat mask with
carved features, painted black hair,
unjointed cloth body
Not marked

About the Doll

The "Kukeri" or ritual dancers of spring are among the most interesting Bulgarian dolls to collect. In a 1940 issue of "Doll Talk", Kimport lists along with their usual Bulgarian dolls "a 'Mummer' with goat-head mask, cow-bell and strange costume" for $6.50. I suspect that only the most curious of collectors probably discovered this wonderful fellow and ordered him. We are lucky to have stumbled into one of their collections!

Costume Description

Spring ritual of KUKERI (plural): separate wood and feather mask; red and black checked jacket; wide red wool sash; feathers and large bells around waist; black baggy pants and native sandals.

With the sound of their bells, the KUKERI frighten away the evil spirits of the winter.

CANADA

New Brunswick Province, Maritime Provinces

7-1/2" Maker unknown Canada c.1950
Cloth head with painted features, gray wool wig, cloth body over wire armature
Not marked

About the Dolls

"Granny" and "Gramp," the little cloth dolls from New Brunswick in Canada, were imported into the U.S. by Kimport Dolls in the early 1940s. Kimport describes them as "solid and wholesome as New Brunswick villagers." These dolls were available until the mid-1950s and then seemed to disappear, until an issue of Kimport's "Doll Talk" for May-June 1966 notes receiving a dozen pairs and the promise of a few more. Unfortunately, Kimport catalogs never reveal the maker of this charming pair.

Costume Description

Couple in winter wear: all garments of wool. She wears a black bonnet with red and blue flowers; hair in a chignon; pink under sweater; blue-green jacket sweater and skirt; red mittens; red petticoat; rust color muff, and black shoes.

He has a black fedora hat; blue-grey sweater; red mittens; light grey pants; and black shoes.

Native Canadian, Eastern Cree (Algonquian)

About the Dolls

The peg-jointed wooden dolls are typically English of the late Georgian period (about 1790 to 1820), and dressed by Eastern Cree Indians who lived along the Hudson Bay mostly in what is today Canada. The dolls' clothing is transitional, containing elements of traditional Cree costume with very fine and elaborate beading and (porcupine) quillwork, combined with use of the Hudson's Bay Company woolen blankets. The wax over composition baby is a later replacement.

We do not know why these dolls were dressed in Cree costume, or for whom. All we can do is speculate. A few of these dolls exist, mainly in ethnological rather than doll collections. Later examples have also been found. The Hudson's Bay Company, to whom I believe we can tie these dolls, was an English firm. They most likely imported the English-made dolls and had them dressed by some of the local Indian people, but why? Surely it was a bit too early for tourism, so we can guess that the dolls were made for presentation pieces to important company officers, or perhaps to visiting English or other VIPs.

Whatever their origin, the dolls provide a wonderful record of the dress of the Eastern Cree Indians. The male doll is one of the only existing sources for information on male Cree dress of the period; consequently, he is not only a beautiful doll, but an essential ethnographic record.

Costume Description

Eastern Cree winter wear: These costumes demonstrate the early contact with Europeans. Set straight on his head is a red cloth cap of square shape, beaded and ribbon trimmed. An elaborate braid casing of beads and fringe hangs down the back; also a beaded bag; red cloth leggings, loin cloth and sash all beaded or fringed. A navy blue cloth coat is worn under a wonderful leather coat painted in geometric designs; beaded garters and moccasins finish his attire.

Baby would be in a moss-stuffed cradleboard with a front laced cradleboard cover, a Cree characteristic.

Her peaked hood, separate sleeves, dress, blanket and leggings are of red cloth. All are ornamented with beads, fringe, and ribbons. Her braid casings, chest piece, belt, and moccasins are fringed and beaded as well.

7"—16" Maker unknown England (dressed by Eastern Cree Indians, Canada) c.1790-1820

Hand-carved wooden head, inset brown glass eyes, dotted eyebrows and closed mouth, brown human hair, peg-jointed wooden body

Not marked

Courtesy of the Rosalie Whyel Museum of Doll Art

Native Canadian, Iroquois

8" Owanyudane Craft Guild (Iroquois) Ontario, Canada 1980s

Corn husk head with mask openings, no hair, cloth and corn husk-wrapped wire body

Not marked

Courtesy of the Rosalie Whyel Museum of Doll Art

About the Doll

The Iroquois people represent their Husk Face messenger spirit in doll form, its body made entirely of corn husks wrapped around a wire armature. The most intriguing part is the miniature mask, made of braided and coiled corn husks, with corn husk fringe.

Iroquois children traditionally played with dolls made from cornhusks, and this one follows the traditional materials, although it would have never been a play doll.

Kimport Dolls offered Iroquois dolls in the July-August 1982 issue of their "Doll Talk" newsletter. In contacting the Owanyudane Craft Guild Canada, who represented the Six Nations Reserve in Ontario, Kimport obtained some examples of Iroquois dolls. This doll has lost its tag, but most likely comes from that connection.

Costume Description

Husk Face celebrant of the midwinter festival. He represents one of the agricultural spirits.

Husk Face messengers go through the community preceding the False Face dancers. Their dances and ceremonies are to insure good health and cure illness. He wears a Husk Face mask, fringed shirt, pants, bandoleer, yarn sash and garters, and beaded moccasins.

CHINA

About the Dolls

Ada Lum designed dolls in Shanghai until about 1949, when she moved her workshop to Hong Kong. Her doll designs have long been emulated by other cloth doll makers in Hong Kong. Ada Lum's dolls came in a variety of sizes, from 6" to the large 15" to 24" examples shown here. Often the dolls came with extra, nicely-crafted clothing; one doll I have seen came with an entire miniature wardrobe and a parchment scroll which told her story.

Costume Description

Work clothes: The man shows a wide straw hat. His top in blue, hers in red; cotton pants. The most simple and ordinary of Chinese work costume.

The basic cut of the garments, including that of the child, is the same.

Mandarin

15" Maker unknown China
c.1860

Composition nodder-type head on very long cylindrical neck, painted features, painted black hair (male also has human hair queue), unjointed composition body

Not marked

Courtesy of the Rosalie Whyel Museum of Doll Art

About the Dolls

A pair of mid-19th century Chinese dolls, in ruling-class Mandarin dress, which are actually beautifully-crafted nodders. Their long cylindrical necks are counterbalanced in a deep neck hole so that they "nod" or bob up and down when touched. An article called "Chinese Nodders" by Barbara Pickering (*Doll Reader®*, July 1987) reports five Chinese terra cotta dolls with nodding heads, 12" in height, brought to England from China in 1855.

The Wenham Museum in Wenham, Massachusetts has a 24" pair of Chinese nodders, probably created by the same person who made the pair photographed here. Their hand-painted silk fabrics have badly deteriorated, like the clothes on these dolls. The weight of the paint, combined with gold and other metals ground into the paint, was probably the cause.

Costume Description

Mandarin's wife: Her dark maroon wrap skirt is covered by a black satin robe with Mandarin square and cranes. Her embroidery is depicted using paint; her bound feet are molded.

Mandarin — Official of the Chinese Empire: his black hat has a red top; blue robe painted to look like fine weaving; blue satin robe over, with Mandarin square depicting cranes — symbol of longevity. Both hat and shoes are molded.

CHINA

About the Doll

The Door of Hope Mission dolls are amongst the finest and best-loved dolls from China. They were carved by native Chinese wood carvers and dressed by the young girls at the Mission.

The Door of Hope Mission was started in Shanghai in 1900 by five missionary women; its first goal was to rescue Chinese prostitutes who worked in the Foreign Settlement area. The Mission opened its first house in November of 1901. With the help of the Chinese, municipal regulations were changed to limit the age of girls who could enter the brothels to 15; consequently a large number of kidnapped children were freed and found shelter in the Mission's first children's home in 1906. In 1912, the Mission was asked to take in any abandoned children. Their far-reaching work continued until 1977. For more information on this fascinating effort, see Patricia Sullivan Planton's article, "The Door of Hope Reopened" (*Doll Reader*®, Feb/March 1980).

As part of their fund-raising efforts, sets of 25 dolls were created by the Door of Hope Mission, plus others by special order. Mission records document that dolls were made as early as 1902. Early dolls had carved heads with all cloth torsos; later ones (of the 1920s and later) usually had carved wooden hands and sometimes wooden feet.

Kimport offered "Chang the Farmer" in their 1937 catalog, with an intricately-carved braid encircling his head (see detail). Our "Chang" has lost his original hat and wears a modern replacement; the holes in his fists are for carrying a hoe, which is shown in Kimport's illustrations. Notice his hand-carved wooden feet.

Costume Description

Rainy day work dress: his outfit consists of blue cotton shirt and pants, cut in rectangles and squares. The straw cloak is for rainy days.

11" Door of Hope Mission Shanghai, China c.1940

Wooden swivel head, carved and painted features, carved and painted black hair, cloth torso with jointed wooden arms and legs

Not marked

(Tibet) Kham Section, Tibet Province

About the Dolls

Tashi Gyantso, the artist of these large and impressive Tibetan dolls, is a Tibetan exile living high in the mountains of northern India. His major work is carving for Buddhist shrines, and the dolls are a sideline. Jim and Bea McDonald of Kirkland, Washington, purchased this pair of dolls when they traveled to India in about 1975. They are still in contact with Tashi, who would make more dolls, but has no way to get them out of his rather remote mountain village and to a post office so that they can be sent to the United States. Otherwise, this author would already own a pair!

An article in *Dolls* magazine in September/October 1989 by Kim Yeshi told of a doll-making project started amongst exiled Tibetan monks living in nearby Nepal. The monks carve the beautiful heads and limbs of the dolls and attach them to cloth bodies. Yeshi gathers silk fabrics for the clothing, also made by the monks. The resulting dolls, featured in this article, are quite astounding. Tashi Gyantso's work, although not part of this project, is in the same tradition.

Costume Description

Her hair in braids; headdress and jewelry in

Tibetan woman, early 20th century. Tibet is now a province of China.

mock silver, coral, and turquoise. Stand collar silk shirt with side opening; black silk robe; pants and cloth boots, lower portion molded.

Summer clothing: man's hair in one long braid; one elongated bead earring; bead necklace; sword; black silk robe (CHUBBA or CHUPA) slung over one shoulder; blue and white pants; cloth boots, lower portion molded.

The country is divided into three parts: Kham, Amdo, and Utsang.

36" Tashi Gyantso Dehra Dun, India c.1975
Papier-mâché shoulder head with painted features, black string wig, hard-stuffed cloth body, cloth arms over wire armature, papier-mâché lower arms
Not marked
Jim and Bea McDonald collection

COLOMBIA

About the Doll

Dolls from Colombia are not frequently seen, especially any well-made ones. The author has a nice cloth example brought back from a trip in the 1980s, plus this somewhat earlier child doll. The celluloid-like plastic body is nice quality, and the hair is an interesting mix, part painted and part black string. She has no marks and has lost any original identification tags.

Costume Description

Hair in two braids tied with ribbons; a black head kerchief covered by a small white knit hat; white cotton blouse, frill at neck and elbows; black gathered skirt with bright ribbon trim; rope sandals with canvas tops tied with black ties.

11" Maker unknown Colombia
c.1950s-1960s
Celluloid-like plastic head with painted features, painted black hair with black string braids, celluloid-like plastic body, jointed at shoulders and hips
Not marked

COSTA RICA

13" Maker unknown
Costa Rica 1940

Cloth head with hand-painted features, black wool wig, cloth body with swing-jointed limbs

TRINA (embroidered on apron)

Courtesy of the Rosalie Whyel Museum of Doll Art

About the Dolls

From a small Central American country with very little tradition of folk costume dolls comes this very charming pair that we found very late in our search! Thanks again go to Jane and Sarah Gregory for their wonderful collection (donated to the Rosalie Whyel Museum). This pair of Costa Rican dolls was purchased in 1940 by Fearn Brown, author of *Dolls of the United Nations*, from Señor Pedro Freer G. of San José. Mr. Freer told Brown that the dolls "represent folk of the country, Spanish and Indian." Unfortunately, Mr. Freer did not record who made these delightful dolls.

Their cloth bodies are stuffed with straw; their faces are sweetly painted onto cloth heads pressed into a mold. Their feet may be the bare feet of country peasants, but their toes (and fingers) are stitched with a festive red embroidery thread!

Costume Description

Her hair in braids and she wears: a black neck band; maroon neckerchief with green stitching; short sleeved pink blouse; white floral print skirt; lace edged petticoat and pantalettes, and bare feet. White apron with TRINA on it.

He wears: a woven straw hat; maroon cotton neckerchief and sash embroidered in green; light grey striped shirt and dark grey striped pants; bare feet.

Bratina-Kupinec (south of Zagreb)

15-1/2" Maker unknown
Croatia c.1960s

Cloth head, painted features, brown floss wig, cloth body with jointed legs, felt arms with separate fingers

Not marked

About the Doll

The authors have seen only one other example of a doll by this maker, and would be very interested in any information on her or him and more examples, please! Obviously, from the large size of the doll (15-1/2") and quality of the workmanship, she was relatively expensive when purchased new, which accounts for the relative scarcity of these dolls.

Her large hands are those of a woman who has known hard work all her life; her body is large and substantial as well. Dressed in her lovely festive costume, she plays an antique lithographed doll-sized accordion and glances coquettishly at her admirers. An utterly charming doll!

Costume Description

Married woman. All garments hand woven in red geometric designs on white: cap, blouse, the sleeveless dress which is tied at the shoulder, laced in front, and pleated except under the apron (which is plain); black leather sandals called OPANKI (plural). She may have red coral beads or, more common is a multicolored necklace and many decorative beads sewn onto her cap.

CROATIA

(Dalmatia) Orebic, Peljesac Peninsula

11-1/2" Armand Marseille Koppelsdorf, Germany
c.1900
Bisque socket head, inset brown glass pupiless eyes,
open mouth with teeth, blonde mohair wig in two
braids down back, ball-jointed composition body
1894 // A.M. DEP. // GERMANY // 7/0

About the Doll

Armand Marseille supplied vast undressed
quantities of their ubiquitous #390 mold (as
well as other molds such as this #1894) to various countries. There the dolls were dressed in
various folk costumes by other companies to
sell to tourists. As late as the 1940s, Kimport
was still obtaining examples of these bisque-
head dolls in various ethnic dress to sell in their
catalogs.

Our doll's missing Florentine hat, kerchief and
jacket are shown on this lady from Croatia.

With renewed interest in the medium of bisque for modern dolls, some countries are
once again importing contemporary bisque-head dolls, this time from the Orient, and
dressing them to sell to tourists.

Costume Description

Red bow in hair; she is missing a small Florentine straw hat with an ostrich feather
over a decorative silk kerchief; small kerchief at neck; blouse of white cotton or silk; brocade bodice could be of a different color and pattern. She also usually has a brocade open
sleeved jacket. The pleated skirt, called KOTULA (singular), is by tradition blue and red
with an ochre yellow section between (here missing). The skirt was padded at the hips
and worn over hoops. The women of this area were the wives of wealthy sea faring men
and wore rich foreign materials and jewelry.

12" Maker unknown Czech Republic c.1960s

Composition swivel head, painted features, brown floss hair, cloth body with disc-jointed arms and legs

Not marked

Courtesy of the Rosalie Whyel Museum of Doll Art

Bohemian Forest, Bohemia

About the Doll

A pleasant Czech girl from Bohemia, an area of the Czech Republic well-known for its products from glassware to beer. The most frequently seen Czech doll costumes are the more ornate, fancy ones from Moravia. The costumes of Bohemia are considerably more subdued and finding a doll from there is a bit of a challenge.

A German brochure about Czech folk art pictures dolls like this one in four different Czech costumes including Bohemia. The brochure is undated but appears to be from the 1950s or '60s. The name of her maker is (somewhat predictably) not mentioned and leaves us, once again, with a mystery.

Costume Description

Unmarried girl: black kerchief with multicolored embroidery in one corner; white cotton blouse, puff sleeve with ruffle at neck and elbow; gathered wool skirt; silk kerchief worn over the black satin bodice which is laced in red; wide floral brocade apron ties hanging down the back. Nearby CHODSKO has a more decorative but very similar costume characterized by an elaborate pleated skirt, and to the south DOUDLEBY has a nearly identical attire.

Bohemian woman showing her embroidered head kerchief, Czech Republic, c.1930s.

CZECH REPUBLIC

(Female) Hluk village; (Male) Vlcnov, both near Uhersky Brod, Moravia

About the Dolls

The end of socialism in the former Czechoslovakia (now Czech and Slovak Republics) has brought widespread change and subsequent privatization of business. Information on former companies such as Slovak Home Industries — difficult to obtain under the best of circumstances, appears to be lost to posterity.

Slovak Home Industries, called "Slip," made Czech and Slovak costumed dolls in the 1930s and '40s with composition heads and cloth bodies. This boy and girl pair are typical "Slip" dolls, pretty but simple figures on which to drape the flamboyant embroideries and laces of the Moravia region. These were the tourist dolls of the period, and are found in the costumes of a number of different regions and towns.

Costume Description

Her hair in one long braid; festive crown of flowers and tinsel with floral ribbons down the back; pleated and starched blouse with black, yellow and red embroidery at the shoulder, the puff sleeve ends in a lace frill

tied with pink ribbon; separate wide lace collar; black pleated sateen skirt is very small, edges covered by the wide brocade apron. The brocade bodice has three bright pompons on the back. Ribbon belt has the same trim as on the bodice. The area along the Moravian-Slovak border is very rich in fabrics and ornamentation.

Festive attire: black felt hat decorated with ribbons, flowers, sequins, and tinsel; full sleeved shirt embroidered on chest, shoulders, and cuffs, in peach and beige; black wool vest and pants with yellow embroidered hearts and vibrant pompons front and back; pants embroidered in blue chain stitch-front only. Yellow embroidered black belt wound around the body three times, and black boots.

Many pictures show men in this costume in the Ride of the Kings at Whitsuntide.

10-1/2—11" Slovak Home Industries Czech Republic c.1939

Composition head with painted features, brown floss hair, cloth body with disc-jointed arms and legs

SLIP // MADE IN CZECHOSLOVAKIA // SLOVAK HOME INDUSTRIES

Courtesy of the Rosalie Whyel Museum of Doll Art

Moravian couple in festive dress, Czech Republic, c.1920s.

CZECH REPUBLIC

Kyjov Region, Moravia

About the Doll

What a jewel this lifelike and rare German character doll is, in the collection of the Rosalie Whyel Museum of Doll Art. A note with the doll says that she was dressed about 1910 in Czechoslovakia (today the Czech and Slovak Republics) for opera singer Marie Cavanova.

The reputed date of 1910 for this doll is certainly appropriate; she is one of the early character-style dolls created in Germany in response to a strong doll reform movement. Artists, craftspeople and parents argued that dolls needed to be more realistic, more childlike — have more "character." It is intriguing that both parents and children, when given what they wanted by doll makers, rejected most of the very realistic dolls (like this one), making them very rare today. The character dolls that they accepted, which consequently are the ones most often found today, generally have much sweeter or more pleasant featured faces.

Maria Cavanova's doll has a delightful costume of Kyjov in Moravia; compare her to the actual child's costume also pictured here.

Costume Description

Best costume: A large red kerchief with a black center would be worn over this white under bonnet (this should be tied in back); white puff sleeve blouse with embroidered frill; red and white striped skirt; blue bodice banded in red, ornamented with embroidered ribbon and sequins; embroidered black apron with lace edge at the lower border; a waist ribbon.

The skirt may also have flowers embroidered among the stripes, or flowers only. Aprons may be more elaborate in nearby areas. There are several costumes from Moravia, including that of Ratiskovice, that are very similar.

20" Swaine and Company Huttensteinach, Germany c.1910

Bisque socket head with painted intaglio eyes, painted features, brown mohair wig in braided oval circlet at back, ball-jointed composition body

F.P. // (impressed on head) GESCHUTZ // S & CO. // GERMANY (green circular stamp back of head)

Courtesy of the Rosalie Whyel Museum of Doll Art

Czech girl's costume from Kyjov, Moravia, early-mid 20th century.

DENMARK

(Left to Right) Aebeltoft, Jutland, Mols Peninsula; Stranby neighborhood, East Funin Island, Odense County; Samso Island, Sjaelland Island group

About the Doll

The discovery of yet another example of these delicate dolls — this time marked "Ingeborg Nielsen, Copenhagen" — finally revealed their maker's name. Letters to a number of experts on Danish dolls led to no information on, or knowledge of, Ingeborg Nielsen. We were about to give up on her as another unsolved mystery!

However, a conversation with friend, librarian, and fellow collector Margaret Groninger sent her digging in her files. She came up with five different references to Ingeborg, ranging from magazine advertisements of the 1940s to doll lists from the 1960s. Thanks to Margaret, the talented Ingeborg Nielsen is "rediscovered"!

Nielsen's 10" dolls are described in the various advertisements as hand-modeled, covered with stockinet and hand-painted; her Danish dolls listed are from Skovshoved and Hedebo, plus a miller in work clothes, and a peasant couple on wooden bench — a grandmother knitting and her mate reading the Bible. An illustration in *House Beautiful*, December 1941, shows Nielsen's couple from Iceland. The three dolls photographed here are part of a collection of ten in different Danish regional costumes.

Ingeborg Nielsen's dolls were imported by the Krug International Doll House in Baltimore and by Velvalee Dickinson of New York City.

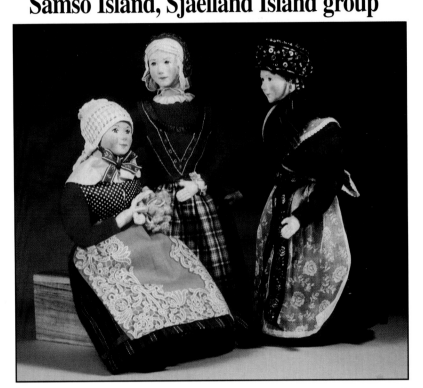

A Danish girl in the dress of Mols. *Courtesy Nationalmuseet, Copenhagen.*

Costume Description

Left: Girl circa 1820-1830: white drawn-work cap with black top, tied with green braid ties; vertically gathered striped woven skirt, ribbon near lower border and no gathers under the apron; neckerchief of white lawn tucked into bodice; red sweater; blue and white dotted bodice; red print apron reflects Rococo influence. She carries flowers of the flax plant made of thread and wool.

Middle: Sunday attire circa 1810-1820: under cap with white lace edge; red over cap with gold braid, red ribbon in back and ties under the chin; white frill at neck and cuff of the blouse; red knitted long sleeved sweater; red wool bodice with peplum, green pleated trim at neckline, white V-shaped embroidery; vertically striped skirt with blue ribbon near hem; very full plaid apron.

Almost an exact replica of Fig. 29 in Ellen Anderson's *Folk Costumes of Denmark.*

Right: Bridal attire of mid-19th century: beaded and sequined black velvet headdress, ribbon in back; wine color, tone on tone, brocade dress with leg-of-mutton sleeves; under shawl of white patterned organdy; over shawl of plaid, both crossed over chest and tied in back; wide white floral organdy apron; black decorative waist ribbon with bow in front; blue and white checked petticoat. Costume was most likely modeled from *Folk Costume in Denmark* by Ellen Anderson, Fig. 7.

Samso bride, left; married lady, right. *Courtesy Nationalmuseet, Copenhagen.*

10" Ingeborg Nielsen Copenhagen, Denmark c.1940s
Pressed stockinet head with hand-painted features, yarn wig, stockinet over wire armature body
SELSKABET TIL // HAANDARBEIDETS // FREMME" (cloth tag sewn under skirt. Province represented by costume is hand-written on tag)

DOMINICA

About the Doll

The bright, tropical sounds and danceable rhythms of a Caribbean steel band — this lively fellow certainly conjures them up! He was created by a local craft factory in Roseau on the island of Dominica. "Tropicrafts" was developed out of an industrial training school for girls, run by Catholic nuns.

Tropicrafts also made woven mats, shopping bags, and sun hats that, like our dolls, were woven from local grasses. In 1984, when Mary Hathaway wrote an article on West Indies dolls (*National Doll World*, March/April 1984), the factory employed 75 women and made ten different types of dolls. The dolls are not marked in any way, so it is fortunate that Hathaway has documented the maker of these distinctively Caribbean dolls.

Costume Description

Drummer: straw hat with red tassel; shirt with French cuffs; colorful fringed sash; stripe down side of pants.

11-1/2" Tropicrafts Roseau, Dominica 1960s

Cloth head with painted features, black yarn wig, woven straw body with braided straw arms

Not marked

Steel drum band from the Caribbean, mid 20th century.

ESTONIA

Vana Mustjala, Saaremaa Island

About the Doll

According to an Estonian friend, this spinning doll was probably made by an Estonian woman in a refugee camp in Geislingen, Germany after World War II. My friend, Taime, was in the camp but cannot remember the name of the doll maker. People in the camp made things to sell to soldiers and tourists. What reveals the doll's origins are the stripes of the skirt, which are embroidered rather than woven because the refugee maker could not obtain woven material from her homeland.

Costume Description

Festive dress: stiffened headdress sequined and embroidered in red, blue and green. Earlier the stiffening was from the bark of trees. Cream silk full sleeved blouse with wide collar (silk is unusual); three conical pins representing sun symbols close the blouse; woven sleeveless dress in orange and cream wool imitated here with braid and embroidery, and red and white braid belt.

12" Maker unknown Possibly Geislingen, Germany (Estonian refugee camp) c.1945-48

Pressed stockinet head, painted features, silk eyelashes, blonde mohair wig, papier-mâché torso, stockinet over wire armature arms and legs

Not marked

Estonian doll, late 1940s, with other folkloric artifacts. She was probably created by the same maker as the doll above.

FINLAND

(Left to right): Kirkkonummi; Finland; (Male) Munsala

About the Dolls

One of the dainty all-rubber dolls from Finland pictured here was found in a plastic cylinder marked "Turun Martta-Nukketeollisuus// Made in Finland," establishing a connection to the "Martha/Martta" (Martta means Martha in Finnish) who made our composition and cloth Laplanders on the next page. Also, there is a probable connection to the composition-head dolls named "Martta" (not illustrated) sold by Kimport in the 1930s and '40s.

Although the styles of the dolls are quite different, the Lapland pair are probably examples of earlier and more labor-intensive works by the doll maker Martta; these later rubber dolls by her successful company were mass-produced and corners had to be cut. But many of her ele-ments of quality and fineness of scale were never sacrificed over the years of production.

Costume Description

Blue cap with lace edge; long white cotton blouse; shoulder ker-chief; bodice; striped woven skirt; white apron; white painted stockings and black shoes.

Man in blue cap; white cotton shirt fastened with pin; red vest with gold buttons; blue knee pants; white painted stockings; black shoes.

The blue bodice, cap, and skirt indicate MUNSALA. The floral print shoulder kerchief, green bodice and red and green striped skirt indicate KIRKKONUMMI.

8-1/2" Martta (Martha) Nukketeollisuus, Finland 1960s
Rubber head, painted features, mohair wig (females), painted hair (male), rubber body with wire armature
TURUN MARTTA—NUKKETEOLLISUUS // MADE IN FINLAND (on bottom of plastic cylinder container)

FINLAND

Lapland

About the Dolls

The early Laplander pair by the doll maker Martta of Abo-Turku, Finland (later of Nukketeollisuus) are very desirable dolls. Here are all of the hallmarks of fine dolls of the period: quality, detail, an intriguing subject and a charming presence.

Hopefully, more research will yield information on the maker and her Finnish dolls. These early Lap dolls are not easy to find, but are well worth the search.

Costume Description

Summer attire: The Lapps live above the Arctic Circle in Finland, Norway, Sweden, and Russia. Their herds of reindeer and the climate shape their lives. Woolen cloth is worn by both men and women in the form of a dark blue tunic decorated with bright colored bands; caps of different shapes for both; pants worn underneath; short fur reindeer boots. In the winter similar garments of reindeer skin are worn.

13" Martta (Martha) Abo-Turku, Finland c.1930s
Composition swivel head with painted features, brown mohair wig, cloth body with swing-jointed limbs
MARTHA-MARTTA-ABO-TURKU // LAPPALAI-NEN POIKA (paper tag) (Female doll reads LAPPALAI-NEN TYTTO) KEKO-MADE IN FINLAND (cloth tag)
Courtesy of the Rosalie Whyel Museum of Doll Art

Young people from Lapland, c.1920s.

FRANCE

Cannes Commune, Alps-Maritimes Department

8" Maker unknown (celluloid doll by Petitcollin) France 1950s

Celluloid one piece head and torso, painted features, dark brown mohair wig, celluloid body jointed at shoulders and hips

(EAGLE HEAD LOGO) // FRANCE // 175

11" Les Poupées Magali (celluloid doll by Société Nobel Française) Nice, France c.1950s

Celluloid swivel head, painted features, black synthetic wig, celluloid body jointed at shoulders and hips

FRANCE // S.N.F. (IN DIAMOND) // 20

Cannes Commune, Alps-Maritimes Department

About the Dolls

Celluloid dolls imported from France are shown in the early 1940s Kimport catalogs, and continued to be made in France into the 1960s (long after the use of flammable celluloid was prohibited in the U.S.). The French celluloid makers of Petitcollin, Société Nobel Française and a few lesser-known makers sold undressed dolls to companies in various cities (of France and of the French protectorates from Martinique to Vietnam) to dress in regional costumes.

One of the companies who dressed celluloid dolls was "Les Poupées Magali," maker of our larger doll on the right. Poupées Magali was the largest producer of French costume dolls in the southeast of France, specializing in the costumes of Provence, the coast and the Principality of Monaco. They used dolls made by the Société Nobel Française as well as Ets. G. Convert. Their dolls' darker color is appropriate for the Mediterranean regions which they represent. (See Elisabeth Chauveau, *Poupées & Bébés en Celluloid.*)

The smaller unmarked doll on the left is by an unknown maker.

Costume Description

This modern costume is almost identical to that of Nice, Monaco, and Liguria in Italy. A rather flat straw hat with felt floral appliqué; gold cross on chain or black ribbon; a short or long sleeved blouse with lace edging and red or black ribbon ties. Nowadays the skirt is of a gathered red and white vertical stripe with black band or bands near the hem; minimal bodice in black. The black neckerchief and apron may match. Earlier a white lace cap was worn under the hat, and the costume had more variety and distinction.

French celluloid dolls by Les Poupées Magali, 1950s

Two charming French women in Alps-Maritimes costume, 1950s.

Flat straw hat embroidered with flowers and place name, Nice, France. Mid 20th century.

FRANCE

Geispolsheim (south of Strasbourg), Alsace Region (modern departments of Bas-Rhin & Haut-Rhin)

About the Doll

Madame Le Minor was a French designer from Pont L'Abbe (in Brittany) who purchased dolls, designed and produced their costumes, and marketed them under her name. Mainly known for the Breton costumes of her native region (illustrated here in a Le Minor catalog page), she also produced dolls of other French provinces such as this young lady from Alsace, as well as other countries and historical models.

Le Minor's first dolls were produced for the World's Fair in 1937, meeting with great approval and success. The dolls from this period, like our Alsatian lass, were composition-head dolls from a German maker, but this type was cut off by World War II. After the War, Atellier Le Minor began to use celluloid dolls made in France, mainly the ones by Petitcollin, but also those of the Société Nobel Française.

Costumes were researched and produced in doll size as accurately (and ornately) as possible; the dolls were each given a name from their region (such as "Lis'l from Geispolsheim in Alsace"). The diamond-shaped gold wrist tag with black printing was used throughout much of the production; later dolls from the 1960s have a sticker with the Le Minor logo.

Madame Le Minor's company ceased production of dolls in 1980. (See Chaveau, *Poupées & Bébés en Celluloid* for more information on this prolific doll maker.)

Costume Description

A cap with a large bow attached and tied under the chin; usually in red or black and includes a red, white, and blue rosette tucked in the bow; gold cross and gold hoop earrings; white organdy puff sleeve blouse; red felt skirt with floral band near hem; black or white fringed shawl, can be floral as well; bodice of black velvet with plastron; apron of pink and silver brocade; a waist ribbon of brocade tied in front bow.

Earlier the colors of the cap and skirt had religious significance; red bow for Catholics and black for Protestants. The skirts were green for Protestants, red for Catholics, and mauve for Jewish. This is now mostly in disuse. Earlier, greater variety existed for this costume which, after the return of the region to France from Germany in 1919, tended to become more and more like the costume around Strasbourg.

Girl holding her French doll in the costume of Alsace, c.1910.

Le Minor doll wrist tag.

A page from Le Minor's catalog illustrating dolls from Brittany, 1930s.

Opposite page:

13" Le Minor Pont l'Abbé, France c.1930

Composition shoulder head, painted features, heavy eye shadow and bright red lips, brown mohair wig, cloth body with swing-jointed arms, celluloid lower arms

JE M'APPELLE [my name is] // LIS'L // MON PAYS EST [my region is] //GEISPOLSHEIM // ON ALSACE (gold wrist tag)

FRANCE

(Female) Kerfeunteun, Quimper Arrondissment, Finistère Department, Brittany Region; (Male) Scaer, Morbihan Department, Brittany Region

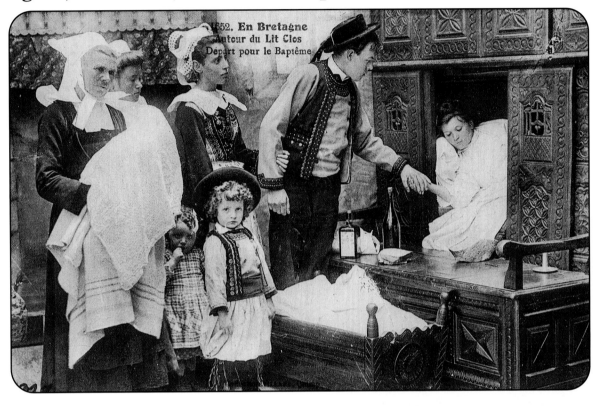

Brittany folk, 1920s. Note the bed, which the doll furniture below emulates.

About the Dolls

A gorgeous pair of French fashion-type dolls of the 1870s or 1880s who have survived together through the years. They represent different small towns of the vastly colorful and unique region of Brittany in France.

Both dolls have pale early bisque heads, subtly-tinted with rose, and gusseted kid leather bodies. It is certainly lucky that their former owners (and now, definitely, their present owner!) treasured the original and beautiful regional costumes.

Costume Description

Festive female attire: white lace cap; blue silk apron trimmed in rust and gold braid; white lace blouse; black bodice-with-sleeves with same trim as skirt and apron; gold cross; black pleated skirt bordered in red, yellow, and silver braid; white stockings and wooden shoes. The odd squares on the chest, trimmed in sequins and lace called SCAPULAIRES (plural) are a clue to the KERFEUNTEUN costume.

Festive male attire: a medium broad-brimmed black felt hat with ribbon band should be worn (furry hat is incorrect); white shirt underneath; black wool vest and navy blue jacket are embroidered in gold colored thread and ornamented with large silver buttons; baggy black wool pants and matching leggings finish this costume.

Doll-sized bed made in Quimper, France. Early 20th century.

Left:	Right:
15" Maker unknown France c.1880s	16-1/2" Eugene Barrois Paris, France 1880s
Bisque swivel head on shoulder plate, inset brown glass eyes, blonde mohair wig, kid leather gusset-jointed body	Bisque swivel head on shoulder plate, inset blue glass eyes, blonde mohair wig, kid leather gusset-jointed body
Not marked	No visible marks
Pat Foster collection	*Pat Foster collection*

FRANCE

Bourg-de-Batz, Loire-Atlantique Department, Brittany Region

About the Dolls

The early dolls by S.F.B.J., a conglomerate of French doll and toy makers called the Société Française de Fabrication de Bébés et Jouets, rode a wave of French dominance in the arts and in fashion. Formed to cut costs and compete with the German doll industry, the French doll society could still not help but flaunt the beauty of their costuming, from these elaborate Breton costumes to very chic little children's frocks.

An elegant pair of early period S.F.B.J. dolls don festive costumes from Bourg-de-Batz in Brittany. Their garments are sewn of silk and soft wool, embellished with tinseled gold, and authentic — down to the "his and hers" embroidered socks. One could only wish that he still had his original very peculiar hat, as shown on the doll in the postcard.

Costume Description

Late 19th-early 20th century female Sunday dress: On the head is a black roll with a white net over it. She is missing a white lace cap that would go over the head and fall onto the shoulders, ornamented with ribbons and at times flowers. Separate white lace collar tied with red ribbon; undergarment in red wool; cream satin cuffs with yellow embroidery and sequins. Dark blue wool sleeveless dress, with trim on top and near the skirt border of black, ochre, and red stitching on black velvet bands. Stiff gold braid plastron, red rosettes at top. Lace edged white silk apron trimmed with gold braid. White silk sash with same trim plus gold fringe and a red flower. Her red knitted knee socks are embroidered in green and gold.

Male Sunday attire: there is a very similar costume in nearby Saille and Guerande. The black felt hat is not original to this costume. The spectacular headwear is a wide brimmed, black felt three cornered hat, ornamented with bright ribbons. Separate wide lace collar tied with red ribbon; white cotton pleated and lace shirt; two vests: white wool under vest trimmed with red ribbon, gold buttons, and buttonholes in green, yellow and blue; the next vest is of moss green wool, embroidered in yellow. Black wool jacket, gold buttons, and yellow embroidery. Very full white pleated pants called BRAGON BAS. Yellow and red embroidery on stockings. Most pictures of this costume show the wonderful hat (already mentioned), colorful ribbon garters and even more vests.

Opposite page & Above:

15"—16" Société Française de Fabrication de Bébés et Jouets Paris, France c.1900

Bisque socket head with blue glass sleep eyes, brown mohair wig, ball-jointed composition/wood body

DEPOSE // S.F.B.J. // 4 (back of head)

Pat Foster collection

Her doll wears the man's special hat from Bourg-de-Batz in Brittany, France, 1911.

FRANCE

Pont-Aven, Finistère Department, Brittany Region

About the Doll

Pont-Aven, with its distinctive lace headdress, is one of the best known and most frequently seen Breton costumes. This lovely celluloid lady from Les Poupées du Venthievre, one of the many doll companies that challenged the pre-eminence of Madame Le Minor, was our choice to illustrate. Many other fine examples of dolls from Pont-Aven exist.

Costume Description

Festive wear: white lace cap with pink ribbons down the back; goffered wide collar lace edged; burgundy velvet long sleeved dress decorated with floral ribbon and gold braid; pink satin pinner apron (a pinned on apron), ribbon, gold braid and lace additions. This costume can appear with even more decorative elements on dress and apron. There can be a bow at the waist either separate or as apron ties.

14" Les Poupées Du Venthievre (celluloid doll by Petitcollin) France 1950s

Celluloid socket head with painted features, brown mohair wig, celluloid body with jointed limbs

LES POUPEES // DU VENTHIEVRE // BRETAGNE (wrist tag)

Late 19th-early 20th century French woman's attire from Pont-Aven.

FRANCE

Pont l'Abbé, Finistère Department, Brittany Region

About the Doll

Another creation by Atelier Le Minor of France was the "Breton Bébé," or Brittany baby. These dolls had a celluloid shoulder head, and soft stockinet body with simple mitten hands, and feet shaped by inserting a cardboard doll shoe sole into the cloth tube. A gold-colored medallion around their neck bears a stylized ermine and "Breiz Bepred" (Brittany Liberated) or "Le Minor" underneath. A particularly lovely and special example of these "Breton Bébés," this one all of celluloid, was presented to General Eisenhower in 1944 in honor of the Liberation of France.

Costume Description

The dress of this Breton Bébé is most similar to Pont l'Abbe. Special gold medallion on gold braid; red taffeta lace-edged bonnet with gold sequins and braid, red bow under chin; cream gathered dress, blue puff sleeves, lace cuffs and Bertha collar. Decorative elements are comprised of gold soutache and braid, also red floral ribbon.

Silk baby cap from Brittany, most likely Pont L'Abbé, circa 1930.

11" Le Minor (celluloid head by Petitcollin) Pont l'Abbé, France 1950s
Celluloid shoulder plate with painted features, open/closed mouth, painted brown hair, stockinet body with stitched mitten hands, cloth over cardboard feet
(EAGLE HEAD) // FRANCE (head) BREIZ // (STYLIZED TREFOIL & ERMINE) // BEPRED (medallion)

Normandy Region

About the Doll

The French company "Les Poupées Cadette" must have been rather prolific, due to the number of dolls found with this label. This lovely lady is the largest example, and has her original box. We have not yet, unfortunately, been able to locate any information on this company.

Although her head and body look deceptively like composition, they are actually painted plastic. Smaller dolls have been found in all celluloid. The overall look is like those dolls by Le Minor (most of the makers of French regional costume dolls of this period emulated her), but the faces are entirely different and the costumes are not as ornate. This large-sized (15") doll even has sleep eyes (a feature not normally found on dolls by Madame Le Minor). Her Normandy coif dominates her costume, and has truly reached remarkable heights!

Costume Description

White winged headdress represents the starched lace coif called BOURGOIN. Gold cross on chain; lilac rayon dress with cuffs and hem decorated with floral ribbon; kerchief with white organdy and gold lace edging; pink taffeta pinner (pinned on) apron; tall headwear of this type is related to the historical hennin (a tall conical headdress).

15" Les Poupées Cadette France 1950s

Painted plastic socket head, sleep eyes with lashes, brown mohair wig, painted plastic body with jointed limbs

LES POUPEES CADETTE // MADE IN FRANCE (paper label on dress)

One of the tall headdresses of
Normandy, France, c.1910.

GAMBIA

Wolof people (probably Muslim; costume similar to Senegal)

About the Doll

Yet another example of a doll by the German firm of Armand Marseille, and this one helps prove how versatile the doll maker really was. This character style baby is an unusual mold number (#362) by itself; to have her wonderful Gambian costume and to know who made it is a rare treat, indeed. A note that came with this doll explains that she was dressed by the "Busy Bees," a young girl's group probably sponsored by missionaries in Gambia. Her layer after layer of homespun and hand-dyed fabric skirts, topped by a silk tunic, harkens back to our older Senegal doll by Bru on page 132. Some day, dolls like this will be the best record of how a people dressed, giving us insight into how they lived.

Costume Description

Turban; beads; outer robe of navy blue with embroidered panels. Several robes may be worn one over the other, so that they can be seen at the lower border. This fashion is considered stylish.

12" Armand Marseille Koppelsdorf, Germany (costuming: "Busy Bees" girl's club, Gambia) 1930s

Bisque socket head, brown glass sleep eyes, open mouth with teeth, black string wig—coiled in strands, five piece composition bent-limb baby body

A.M. // GERMANY // 362 / 3.K

Gail Hiatt collection

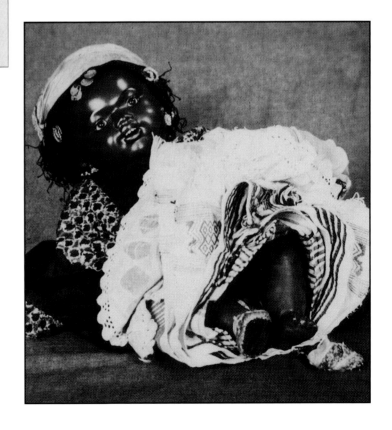

Photography by Dave Duncan.

Hanauer Area (between the Schwarzwald and the Rhine River)

About the Dolls

A small pair of bisque-head dolls produced by the brothers Kühnlenz in Germany, and probably purchased by a tourist in the 1910s or 1920s. The dolls are very detailed for their small size and scale, and are luckily quite well-preserved. The girl's mohair wig is in two braids down her back (see photo detail), a typical trait that can help identify whether a redressed or undressed doll originally wore a German or other European regional costume.

Costume Description

Sunday dress: black felt broad brimmed hat; white pleated shirt; black bow tie; red felt vest closed with gold buttons; long black felt coat faced in red with gold buttons; black felt pants; red ribbon garters. Another instance where felt substitutes for the wool of the actual garments.

Her hair in two long braids; black cap with large bow attached; lace trimmed blouse with red satin elbow ribbons; red (faded in photo) wool gathered skirt with black trim near hem; black velvet bodice, plastron of gold metallic braid and sequins; white lace bordered apron; pale blue waist ribbon. This costume has a strong resemblance to the dress in Alsace across the Rhine River in France.

7-1/4" Gebrüder Kühnlenz Kronach, Germany c.1910s

Bisque socket head, inset brown pupiless glass eyes, open mouth, brown curly mohair wig (female has blonde wig), five piece jointed composition body

G.K. (IN CIRCLE WITH RAYS) // 44.15

Schwalm, Hesse State, southwestern Germany

About the Doll

The German porcelain factory of Simon and Halbig produced lovely, high-quality heads for assembly into dolls by a variety of companies including makers of regional costume dolls. In general, their earliest heads are of the shoulder head variety, some with movable (swivel) heads and some marked (like this doll) with the distinctive "S H" and a size number on the front of the shoulder plate. In this small size, the eyes are glass but set stationary rather than sleeping style, and the petite body is made of cloth rather than leather (probably a cost-cutting measure for the tourist doll). Her wig is braided into a tightly-coiled bun at the back of her head.

She is the type of small bisque doll that tended to get overlooked (thank goodness) in some collectors' and dealers' frenzy to redress dolls in fancier clothing. There is a great variety of these types of small bisque-head dolls to look for, some of them a great bargain, to add to a collection of dolls in regional costume.

Costume Description

Hair brought to top of head into a knot covered by a small red cylinder called a BETZEL (singular), tied on by black ribbons. White short sleeve blouse; black gathered wool skirt with decorative band at hem; multicolored kerchief tucked into black velvet bodice having a red heart-shaped front and tabs; white cotton apron; white stockings; garters at the knee; petticoats include black cotton with a red band and red flannel print with a white band. Real shoes would have large silver buckles. Skirts are very short, very full, and have many petticoats underneath.

10" Simon & Halbig Grafenhain, Germany late 1880s
Bisque shoulder head, brown glass inset eyes, open mouth with four molded teeth, blonde mohair wig in coiled braid on top of head, cloth body and upper limbs, bisque lower arms
S H 2/0 10
Pat Foster collection

Three small Hessian girls dressed much like adults, Germany, 1914.

Gutach, Schwarzwald (Black Forest), Württemberg and Baden States

About the Doll

A hand-carved wooden-head doll with simple but lovely features and interesting braided flaxen hair. Her cloth body is again a study in simple but sturdy construction. She must have been an expensive doll when purchased; I have only seen a few of these dolls photographed or for sale. For several years, I could not find any information on her maker, but recently Laura Knüsli, who is studying wooden dolls, came to my aid. She says that this engaging girl was made by doll artist Anna Fehrle, who began making play dolls with carved wooden heads and cloth bodies during the 1930s. Like Käthe Kruse's dolls, they were stuffed with deer hair and later kapok. After Anna's retirement, probably sometime in the 1950s, her work was continued by her grand-niece Susi Schön. The dolls from this more recent period are stuffed with a synthetic material.

Costume Description

Young woman's festive wear: hair in braids and tucked up; straw hat tied under chin with black felt ribbons hanging down and red pompons covering top of hat; white cotton puff sleeve blouse, ruffles at neck and sleeve; black gathered felt skirt edged in buff felt; black velvet bodice, tiny embroidered flowers front and back; a particular yoke called a HALSMANTEL (singular) goes over the shoulders and has been in recent times joined to the bodice. Medium blue apron with blue cord ties. A sheer black undercap is not always shown on dolls. This is worn indoors and out; when outside, the straw hat is added. Red pompons are for young women and black for matrons. Apron may be blue or green. A red under skirt is generally worn.

Verlag von G. Röbcke, photogr. Kunstanstalt, Freiburg i/B.

Volkstracht aus dem Gutachthal.

D. 3362

Unmarried German ladies in Sunday dress of Gutach, c.1905.

Opposite page:

14" Anna Fehrle workshop Germany 1950s-1960s

Carved wooden swivel head, painted features, blonde flax wig, jointed cloth body, separate thumb and stitched fingers

SEMPLE (small metal wrist tag)

GERMANY

Schwarzwald (Black Forest), Württemberg and Baden States

12-1/2"—14" Ilse Ludecke Germany c.1965
Needle-sculpted cloth head with sculpted ears, painted side-glancing eyes, fur wig, cloth body with swing-jointed arms, wooden base
602 CLOCKMAKER BLACK FOREST ILSE DOLL WESTERN GERMANY (paper tag. Also a paper booklet telling story of "Michel" the clockmaker)

About the Dolls

Ilse Ludecke of Germany started making dolls in the 1940s, selling them to American officers' wives and others. Her early dolls are quite different from "Michel" photographed here. They are quite small (4"-8") and often illustrate fairy tales; their sweetly-painted faces have little circles of rouge on their cheeks. The early dolls are not marked.

Ilse Ludecke's larger regional costume dolls, marked "Ilse," seem to date from a later period, perhaps the 1950s or 1960s. We have seen several different styles from Germany and Holland, plus other countries.

Kimport introduced Michel the clock-maker to collectors in their January-February 1966 issue of "Doll Talk." They wrote that Miss Ludecke was a crafts instructor and had done work for the U.S. Armed Forces in Germany, later becoming a full-time doll maker. Michel was amongst 3,000 entries in the San Francisco Golden Gate doll exhibit in 1965, placing second. Michel sold for a hefty sum of $25 in 1966.

Costume Description

Clockmaker's attire: black felt hat; white cotton shirt with ribbon tie; red felt vest; blue felt jacket with green lining and all buttons represented by sequins; black knee pants; white stockings; black shoes with silver buckles.

He has an umbrella, a bag for possessions, and on his back a board with clocks for sale and an oil cloth to roll down in case of rain. Again, felt representing wool on the doll costume.

Schwarzwald (Black Forest), Württemberg and Baden States

15-1/2" Kämmer & Reinhardt Waltershausen, Germany c.1910

Bisque socket head, painted blue intaglio eyes, dark blonde mohair wig, ball-jointed composition body

K*R // 101 //39

Courtesy of the Rosalie Whyel Museum of Doll Art

About the Doll

The Colemans note a 1912 "Leslie's Illustrated Weekly" which states that the character doll was made to represent Germany and other European countries, before the spread of French fashion. Doll dressmakers were compelled to study museums (and books, which accounts for the similarities of doll costumes to books on the subject published at the time) to produce accurate folk dress. The newspaper comments that dolls of this type have an educational value (Coleman, Dorothy, Elizabeth, and Evelyn J., *The Collector's Encyclopedia of Dolls Vol. Two*, pp. 981-982.).

A large number of the German character dolls, when found in their original clothing, do wear folk costumes of Germany and other parts of Europe. Strong nationalist movements in Germany and other European countries, mixed with a desire for more "natural" looking dolls, led to character dolls dressed in more or less accurate regional costumes. Artists Marion Kaulitz and Käthe Kruse, both involved in the creation of this type of doll, dressed their works in a sturdy "peasant" look in opposition to the frothy French fashions of the time. Kämmer and Reinhardt, a doll company who began the mass production of the character dolls, followed suit.

Our lovely "Marie," a Kämmer and Reinhardt mold #101, wears a fine original example of a costume from Germany.

Costume Description

Black cone shaped hat, bow in back with ends hanging down; red silk blouse; black printed kerchief tucked into the red satin bodice with gold buttons; red pleated skirt, blue ribbons near hem, and brocade apron.

GERMANY

About the Doll

Character dolls, like this unusual mold #550 by Armand Marseille, are often found in regional costumes of Germany (such as our girl from Spreewald) and other countries. It was considered desirable to dress this type of "more natural" doll in either simple children's clothing or in "peasant" costume. The costumes can be fairly elaborate and accurate, done either at the factory or by a seamstress commissioned to do the special costume. It is also a reasonable assumption that this type of doll was rarely intended to be sold in a tourist shop!

Costume Description

Very pale blue stiffened head kerchief called a LAPA (singular), edged in lace, and decorated with ribbon. White short sleeved blouse with lace trim; black velveteen bodice; red silk fichu crossed over bodice; blue pleated cotton skirt with floral band at hem, may also be red or black. The pastel colors of shawl, apron, and headwear may vary. She is missing a pretty white apron and a floral waist ribbon.

Berliners would go to the Spreewald district on a Sunday to partake of the famous eel dishes and cherry pies.

The Wends (Slavic people of eastern Germany) are said to have come to this area about 1,500 years ago.

16-1/2" Armand Marseille   Koppelsdorf, Germany c.1915
Bisque socket head with brown glass sleep eyes, dark brown mohair wig in coiled braids, ball-jointed composition body
Not marked
Courtesy of the Rosalie Whyel Museum of Doll Art

Young Spreewald ladies, wearing aprons like our doll should be wearing, Germany, 1910s.

Luneburg, near Hamburg, Vierlande District, Hamburg State

About the Dolls

The streets of mid-19th century Hamburg were filled with the colorful flower vendors from Vierlande (near Hamburg) dressed in this distinctive costume. According to a note pinned to the doll's skirt, Caroline Fisher succumbed to the charms of this pair of dolls in Vierlande costume in 1852, like any good tourist looking for gifts to take home. Probably bought in a street market, the dolls are of the cheaply and quickly-made papier-mâché variety that were turned out of German factories of the period. It is such a pleasure that Caroline bought both the man and the lady dolls, for the male costumes are far less commonly seen. The dolls' survival in such wonderful condition —despite the loss of the lady doll's unique outer hat — is rare indeed.

Costume Description

The man would wear a black top hat; white long sleeved shirt, pin at neck and a soft kerchief tie; vest can be rather fancy, embellished with buttons; flap front knee pants with buttons; white stockings and black shoes. He could wear a dark colored jacket also with buttons. In fact, the impression is that buttons are this costume's major motif.

This feminine costume is almost always shown with a rather specific round flat straw hat with a bow and ribbon at the back and another bow tied under the chin. Mostly depicted as vendors of flowers and fruits. There is usually a plaid neck kerchief, white blouse, pins at neck, bodice, skirt, blue and white striped apron. Could have a jacket with elliptical front opening and cuff buttons. Our lady has a lace bonnet and a red and gold trimmed bodice.

A flower vendor of Vierlande, near Hamburg, Germany, c.1905

9" Attributed to Andreas Voit Hildburghausen, Germany 1852

Papier-mâché shoulder head with painted features, painted black hair, cloth body with wooden lower arms

BROUGHT FROM HAMBURG BY CAROLINE FISHER 1852 (paper tag pinned to skirt of female doll). Male doll not marked

Courtesy of the Rosalie Whyel Museum of Doll Art

Attica, Attica and Boeotia Departments

About the Doll

What a pleasure to find this French lady doll in a marvelous costume of Greece. The costume is probably not from the factory because it is too meticulously and accurately done; instead, she may have been dressed in Greece for a special occasion or even by a Greek immigrant to another European country or the United States. Her garment seems to have been created from portions of an adult costume (compare it with the detail of an embroidered adult sleeve). It seems to have been with her for a long time, the materials are old, and the quality is very good.

Costume Description

Festive wear: she would wear a diadem and neck piece of metal coins and false gems. A cream color silk veil with sequins and gold fringe would go over the headpiece. These, along with special bracelets, are missing here. She wears a bib necklace of beads and coins which is also worn in Salamis.

Major garment is the heavily embroidered sleeveless chemise or POKAMISO (singular). An embroidered bodice-with-sleeves; a red wool sash; two matching red and white sleeveless coats with gold embroidery are correct for the full sized dress. The woven apron is somewhat unusual; one of white eyelet or none is more common, for best wear. The embroidery is taken from the sleeve of a full sized garment.

These people came out of Albania at an earlier time.

17" François Gaultier Paris, France (costuming) Greece 1880s
Bisque swivel head on shoulder plate, inset blue glass eyes, closed mouth, blonde mohair wig, kid leather body with stitched fingers
Not marked
Pat Foster collection

A piece work textile fashioned of ornamental towels.

20th century embroidered sleeve fragment from Attica, Greece.

GREECE

Attica, Peloponnesus, and much of mainland Greece

10-1/2" Maker unknown
Greece 1930s

Pressed cloth head with painted features, wool wig, cloth body with swing-jointed arms, weighted feet

Not marked

Courtesy of the Rosalie Whyel Museum of Doll Art

About the Doll

This fellow with hand-painted features on a pressed cloth face is an earlier example (circa 1930s) of a style of Greek costume dolls available quite readily to the collector. The early examples are all cloth, with a lot of handwork. Later examples become quite stylized, with bright painting, leggy bodies with small heads, and often gaudy costumes. Examples since the late 1950s have plastic arms. Look around for the older ones to collect, and then consider the facial painting, body construction, and authenticity of dress.

Costume Description

Man's soft red cap with long black tassel; white cotton open sleeve shirt; off white and black embroidered jacket with vestigial sleeves, usually worn hanging down the back; pale blue sash; white gathered lower body garment is called a FOUSTANELLA (singular). It is, at times, compared to the Scottish kilt, but the two are constructed in dissimilar ways and have evolved differently. Long white leggings are kept from bagging by black garters. His footwear, called TSAROUKIA, is of red leather with large pompons. The outfit is frequently called the EVZONE costume. However, the EVZONE Guards wear a ceremonial uniform which is based on the folkloric FOUSTANELLA.

GREECE

Island of Lefkas, Ionian Islands, Preveza Department

About the Dolls

Near East Industries was a division of the Near East Foundation, founded in Greece to help refugees in the Balkans. Dolls made by local Greek artisans and distributed through the Industries were a popular sales item. They were imported into the United States by companies like Kimport, and were good sellers because of their high quality and low price.

Earlier dolls (1920s) from the Near East Industries, represented by our Macedonian girl (page 92), are not easy to find. The later ones (from the late 1930s and 1940s) are illustrated by these three from Greece and elsewhere by a pair from Albania. Small but well-painted and quite lovely, these dolls are readily available to the collector because of the number sold by Kimport and other doll companies. The dolls are also usually quite well-marked; even if the tags have been lost, the dolls are distinctive and very recognizable.

Costume Description

Festive dress: Her hair pulled back into two braids; small black cap tilted to one side and embroidered in silver or gold thread fastened with ornamental hat pins; embroidered white kerchief worn over the cap, and another over the shoulders; white crepe chemise with open sleeve; blue silk sleeveless dress, blue and white thread trim; blue silk sash; silver braid buckle.

She may wear a long coat in the same material as the dress. The colors and fabrics of the dress and coat tend to be rich and without pattern. The kerchief and chemise are nearly always white and are finely embroidered in white. This costume is influenced by European styles.

Festive wear: He wears a black head wrap in a single loop to one side of his head; white shirt; band collar and closed sleeve; black wool braided vest and the famous Island VRAKA (singular) or baggy pants. Blue striped wide sash; leather TSAROUKIA (shoes) with no pompons. He could have a black wool jacket bordered sometimes in blue, slung over his shoulder.

8" Near East Industries Athens, Greece c.1940

Cloth head with hand painted features, floss hair, cloth body, wire-strung arms

NEAR EAST INDUSTRIES // MADE IN // ATHENS, GREECE (cloth tag on underclothes). NEAR EAST INDUSTRIES // MY NAME IS _____ // MY COSTUME IS _____ // PRICE _____ (paper tag on front with names, etc. in ink)

Pair on right: *Courtesy of the Rosalie Whyel Museum of Doll Art*

GREENLAND

Inuit people (Eskimo)

About the Doll

Listed in Elsie Krug's doll newsletter of June 1942 for $25 is a 14" pair of these superb carved wooden dolls from Greenland. This was an extravagant price for almost any doll in 1942; many of the older bisque and china head dolls were selling for the same or less! Is it any wonder that these fine dolls by native Greenland Inuit (Eskimos) are very rarely seen?

Costume Description

Festive attire: wide black silk headband; blue shirt with white bells and green ties; wide beadwork collar; narrow leather belt; fancy embellished fur pants and decorative boots.

Greenlanders wearing their wide bead collars, 1906.

14" Maker unknown Greenland 1930s-1940s

Carved wooden head, carved/unpainted features, brown human hair wig, carved wooden body and limbs

Not marked

Courtesy of the Rosalie Whyel Museum of Doll Art

61

GUATEMALA

Nebaj Village

About the Doll

A friend's trip home to Guatemala brought us some lucky finds including this new (reproduction) doll made by Alice Barrutia-Wynn. Mrs. Barrutia-Wynn is Guatemalan by birth and lived much of her life in the United States. She learned to make bisque dolls here and decided to move back to Guatemala and try teaching the art. It has become a flourishing business for her. Alice hopes to also begin sculpting some original dolls.

Alice's love for the native weaving and embroidery of Guatemala led her to dress her lovely-complexioned dolls (this one a reproduction of an Armand Marseille character child) in various costumes. The costumes are created for her by local women; this one from Nebaj — one of the most colorful costumes of all, resplendent with a uniquely-tied hat — was made especially for this book.

Costume Description

Daily dress: hand-woven head wrapping with tassels; silver bead earrings and necklace; multicolored HUIPIL (singular); red woven cotton wrap skirt; HUARACHES (plural) and a woven belt. The people of Guatemala are famous for a variety of weaving skills.

16" Alice Barrutia-Wynn Guatemala City, Guatemala 1995

Bisque socket head, inset brown glass eyes, open mouth, black synthetic hair in long braid down back, bisque toddler body, jointed arms and legs

Not marked

Modern Guatemalan women making dolls.

Mid 20th century Guatemalan household textile.

GUATEMALA
Totonicapan Department

About the Dolls

Another example of these dramatic and highly unusual dolls resides at the Wenham Museum in Wenham, Massachusetts. She came to the Wenham Museum with a note which read: "Guatemala—[she] makes all the marriages." Lorna Lieberman, curator, calls her an "imposing presence."

A friend born in Guatemala City carried a picture of these dolls home with her, trying to help us find their talented maker. She showed the picture to a gentleman who (apparently) immediately recognized them as the work of don Francisco Arango, Senior. However, there is still some confusion because don Francisco Arango, Senior was famous for his lifelike figures made in wax. Yet these dolls are cloth, and it is not yet known whether this artist also made dolls like these. We are continuing to try to investigate, and hope that we are on the right track to discovering the maker of our splendid Guatemalan pair.

Guatemalan woman showing a
typical headdress, 1904.

Costume Description

She is from San Cristobal Totonicapan. She is arrayed in a white veil over a head wrapping and flowers; an embroidered HUIPIL (singular) covered by a lace over-garment; and a multicolored hand-woven skirt. The frills and ruffles are post conquest additions.

Ceremonial or best clothing: The man has his hair in two braids, over this would be worn a magenta head kerchief (here missing); a white cotton shirt; black jacket; long white underpants covered by black embroidered split-overpants called SOBRE PANTALONES. The ribbons that tie the pants at the ankle are not indigenous.

27" Attributed to don Francisco Arango, Senior Guatemala c.1930s
Pressed cloth head, mask face with painted features, dark brown floss hair, cloth body with swing-jointed arms and legs
Not marked
Courtesy of the Rosalie Whyel Museum of Doll Art

GUINEA

Fulani people

About the Doll

Fearn Brown, in her book *Dolls of the United Nations*, shows a Fulani man and woman by the same maker (ours has become very jealous of Brown's doll because of her handsome male partner). No maker's name is documented, unfortunately.

A lively imagination created this cloth doll, with her elaborate and funky hairstyle. The wealthier women of the Fulani tribe wear much jewelry and other ornamentation plus these hairstyles, built up on bamboo and wire frame, to show wealth and status in their society.

Costume Description

Hair in a very particular style of double loops held in place by bamboo rods. Hair ornaments, bracelets, and neck beads are worn.

Cap sleeved blouse with peplum in several different cotton prints; a blue and white print wrap skirt. The cotton prints vary from person to person so that color and design will change but the garment cut will remain much the same.

14-1/2" Maker unknown Guinea 1960s-1970s

Cloth head, embroidered features, black wool wig in distinctive Fulani hairstyle, cloth body jointed with fabric covered buttons

Not marked

Detail of Guinean hair arrangement.
Courtesy Information Guinea.

Kalocsa Region

About the Dolls

Spilt milk and a curious cat have caused our little girl to plunk herself on the floor and howl in frustration. Older sister kneels with her hanky, waiting for the worst of the tantrum to subside! These two dolls, purchased thousands of miles apart — one in Budapest and one in Philadel-phia, just begged to come together for a photograph.

I am quite positive the crying child is a late but very atypical work

by Marga. Margit (called "Marga") Szere-lemhegyi's dolls, another of which is seen on the next page, are more typically sweet and calm-featured cloth dolls. Although later (after World War II), Marga's dolls had heads of composition, normally even her child dolls retain this unruffled visage. But I have compared this not-so-calm little girl with Marga's other work; her body construction, hair, and clothing are virtually the same. Her thick-soled black leather shoes with blue ribbon ties are the final clue; Marga used this type of shoe on many of her dolls. She must have enjoyed making this so-different, so-stubborn little girl!

The "older sister" doll was purchased in 1995 in the folk arts store in my hotel in Budapest. I had already visited with the doll maker Marika, who makes contemporary cloth dolls in Hungarian costume, so I was not able to confirm my feelings that this doll is one of hers. Marika showed us small dolls that she makes today in costumes of Kalocsa; this one is very similar, but is not marked.

Unmarried (left) and married ladies from Kalocsa, Hungary, 1960s.

Costume Description

Festive attire: hair braided into chignon, blue bow on top of head with ends down the back, indicate a marriageable girl. Married women would have an embroidered cap. Beads at neck; full pleated pastel skirt embellished with white lace edging and a wide lace band worn over many petticoats; white cotton blouse, bodice and apron are satin stitched with typical Hungarian flowers in profusion. Fancy stockings with garters and red mules are worn. The colors of the ribbon and the skirt may be different, but the three or four embroidered garments would remain the same. This seems to be a rather late costume evolvement, coming to bloom in this century. The same embroidery motifs are used to paint the inside house walls. These are painted free hand.

The baby bonnet and diminished embroidery constitute the differences between the little girl and her adult counterpart.

Left:

10" Attributed to Margit Szerelemhegyi ("Marga")
Budapest, Hungary c.1950

Composition head, painted features—closed eyes, crying mouth and molded tears, blonde floss wig, cloth body with disc-jointed limbs, separate fingers, right hand holding metal spoon

MADE IN HUNGARY (stamped on petticoat)

Right:

13" Maker unknown Hungary 1994

Pressed stockinet head, painted features, brown floss wig, stockinet body with cloth over wire armature arms, jointed cloth legs

Not marked

HUNGARY
Mezokovesd, Borsod County

About the Dolls

Probably the best-known and most often represented costume of Hungary is that of Mezokovesd. The postcard shows this fantastical costume from the 1910s; how closely the dolls illustrate it!

The boy doll is very typical of nice (but not grand or expensive) dolls from Hungary from the 1930s until as late as the 1960s. Their composition heads have pleasant smiles and sparkling eyes; the bodies are simple cloth affairs. You can still buy dolls that look very much like him in Budapest today. The fine needlework of the older dolls (seen in his apron) is what sets them apart.

His lady friend is from the hands of the talented Margit Szerelemhegyi (nee Margit Vöros de Magyarbel), whose doll com-

HUNGARY

Mezokovesd, Borsod County

pany was known by her pet name of "Marga." Her fabulous, painstakingly-constructed and detailed dolls are not common because they were quite expensive even in their time. Marga's dolls were shown at the New York World's Fair in 1939. Kimport, in a "Doll Talk" newsletter from 1939, describes the Hungarian booth and some unidentified dolls (definitely by Marga): "those marvelous felt fabric faces, the costumes heavy with rich embroidery, many pleated skirts, real leather shoes and hand-knit stockings—they are so lovely and so rare that they're well-worth the prices asked [$40]."

Lady with a different Mezokovesd headdress holding a typical doll, 1950s. *Hungarian Ethnographic Museum.*

Some of Marga's dolls are marked by a heart-shaped tag bearing the name "Marga." Others like this one bear the names of the cooperative "Hangya" which sold them.

The later Marga dolls have composition heads (see the crying child on page 65) and date from just shortly before World War II. Budapest, like many European capitals, was bombed during the war and left in shambles. Marga's life, like that of other Hungarians, was totally disrupted and her lovely dolls seemed to disappear shortly thereafter.

Back of doll on opposite page.

Costume Description

Male Sunday wear: tall green Derby-like hat with ribbon band; green felt vest decorated with white soutache and sequins. Both hat and vest are more likely to be black. The embroidered shirt has a small collar and wide open sleeves; embroidered black sateen apron ends in fringe. Wide white pants with self fringe called GATYA (singular); black leather boots. All this hand embroidery is in satin stitch.

Married woman's festive dress: the headdress with the distinctive oval front and cone shaped back is worn for the first year of marriage. Another headdress is a large kerchief carrying large condensed pompons, worn by married women. Bead necklace and earrings; floral print blouse with black velvet yoke, puff sleeve and floral ribbon at waist, ends in a peplum. Floral challis sleeveless dress, looks like skirt, pleated until near the bottom, a large portion of which is embellished with braids and trims. Black sateen apron, black fringe border, lower section of multicolored hand-embroidered flowers. The blouse and sleeveless dress may have different colors and prints, but the apron will be, if not the same, very similar. A floral shawl with decorative wool fringe and/or a jacket may also be worn.

Bride and groom from Mezokovesd in Hungary, 1920s.

HUNGARY

18-1/2" Maker unknown Hungary c.1920s

Made from architectural pieces: wooden head with attached metal hat, drawn and painted features, no hair, polychromed wooden body with hinged arms, metal vest

Not marked

Puszta or Great Plain

About the Doll

How curious and captivating this plainsman figure is, representing the Hungarian cowboy. It is difficult to judge how old this doll is, since he is constructed of vintage architectural elements — columns, newel posts and strips of tin with punchwork decoration. His bits and pieces may have been gathered from the remains of old village buildings. Although primitive, he is very dynamic and expressive of a lifestyle even older than the elements from which he was created.

Costume Description

He represents herdsmen or CSIKOS (plural) in working clothes. His hat is a smaller version of the broad black felt hat. A white linen open sleeved shirt, a red vest which is usually black, GATYA (singular) wide white linen pants. Blue apron which would not be worn while riding. The metal oblong pieces stand in for his embroidered SZUR (singular) or great coat.

Hungarian plainsman in his great coat or SZUR.

ICELAND

About the Doll

Dolls from Iceland, especially older ones, require an extensive search to find! This one has a typical 1930s composition head, with heavy eyeshadow, probably made in Germany. Her distinctive braided and looped hairstyle is unique to this Icelandic costume.

Costume Description

Hair in four braids crossed in back and tucked under black velvet hat with long tassel. Gold pin; pink satin apron and long sleeved blouse; full length black gathered skirt; black satin bodice with decorative bodice hooks and gold tinsel belt. This costume's colors are more likely to be dark with white linens, the pink is unusual. There may be a dark colored jacket. There is another more festive dress in black with rich gold embroidery.

Back view of Icelandic costume, showing the typical hairstyle, 1910s.

16" Maker unknown   Iceland   1930s

Composition shoulder head, painted features, light brown mohair wig, cloth torso and legs, celluloid lower arms

Not marked

Noreen Ott collection

INDIA
Lambadi people, Andhara Pradesh State

About the Dolls

Shown here are two intricately-dressed Lambadi women from India by two different doll makers from the 1960s. The cloth doll on the left is from the Christa Seva Mandir Doll-Production Circle (a missionary project or self-help group) from Sholapur in south India. A large paper tag attached to the back of her colorful head veil, describes her region of Andhara and the life of the nomadic Lambadi (or Lambani) peoples. A group of dolls by this maker, from various pradeshes (provinces) of India, have the same distinctive face, body and stance.

On the right is Mrs. Viji Srinivasan's version of a Lambadi woman. She also made the seated dancer from Orissa on the opposite page. Her dolls are quite recognizable, with nicely hand-painted ceramic heads and cloth bodies, cloth over wire arms and long, separated fingers. She "signed" her dolls via an address label under the base.

Costume Description

Draped over the heads of our ladies are multipurpose veils; earrings, bracelets and necklaces in abundance; a close fitting blouse or CHOLI (singular), and a gathered skirt. All the garments with appliqué and mirrors in bright colors.

Note: Andhara and Andhra are both correct spellings.

Left: 9" Christa Seva Mandir Doll Production Circle Sholapur, India 1960s

Pressed cloth head, painted features, black yarn hair, cloth body with swing-jointed arms and unjointed legs

CHRISTA SEVA MANDIR DOLL-PRODUCTION CIRCLE, SIDDESHWAR PETH, SHOLAPUR, INDIA (Descriptive paper tag on back)

Right: 10" Mrs. Viji Srinivasan Madras, India 1963

Ceramic head, painted features and tattoos on face, black mohair wig, cloth body over wire arms, separately stitched fingers and big toe (bare feet)

(inscribed) LAMBADI GIRL // FROM ANDHRA (printed) MRS. VIJI SRINIVASAN // 90, HABIBULLAH ROAD // MADRAS-17 // S. INDIA (paper label under base)

INDIA

(Left to right) Marwari people, Rajasthan State; Savarah people, Orissa State; Maharaja

About the Dolls

India has long produced very pleasing dolls which still tend to be ignored by doll collectors. Perhaps it is because the dolls are plentiful at the present and, due to a certain sameness, are really quite difficult to sort out as to specific makers. Missionary and other self-help groups have long organized crafts like doll making, and the molds (for pressed cloth heads) and body patterns seem to have been passed from group to group. If there is no tag on the doll, it can be almost impossible to know the maker (at least at this point).

The Marwari woman, top left of our circle of Indian dolls, was made by the "poor women and widows" at Nagpada Neighborhood House in Bombay. Her companion, a Maharaja, was produced from a taller version of virtually the same pattern. He is tagged "Khilowna Brand" which I believe to be the name of home industry products by Sont Nathu. Loretta Holz's excellent (but out-of-print) book on international dolls shows a photograph of four dolls by Sont Nathu; some examples of the dolls in her photograph have been found with "Khilowna Brand" tags.

There are a group of somewhat older (c. 1950s) Indian cloth dolls, again made from the same molds and patterns. I have not yet found one tagged. These dolls have the distinction of having finger and toenails painted white, with red lines between each; their clothing is also finer and more detailed.

The seated dancer in our Indian circle is another doll by Mrs. Viji Srinivasan of Madras (she also made the Lambadi woman shown on the previous page). Her head is ceramic, with a cloth body sewn into seated position, cloth over wire arms and long, separated fingers. A noticeable feature of her lady dolls is their ample, very pointed breasts!

Costume Description

Sitting woman: hair in chignon; bead and metal earrings, necklaces and bracelet; red cotton CHOLI (singular) or blouse; and woven cotton sari.

Woman on left: white veil; red CHOLI (singular) (close fitting blouse) with gold trim; wide floral print skirt with red border.

Man on right: green metallic turban; pearl pin and necklace; red satin shirt; red satin coat with gold braid and epaulettes; white cotton pants; red plastic shoes; holding a sword.

*Note: Savarah and Savara are both correct spellings.

Center Front:

7-1/2" Mrs. Viji Srinivasan Madras, India 1960s

Ceramic head with painted features, black wool wig, cloth body, cloth over wire armature arms and legs in seated position, separate fingers

(inscribed) SAVARA WOMAN // —ORISSA
(printed) MRS. VIJI SRINIVASAN // 90, HABIBULLAH ROAD // MADRAS-17 // S.INDIA (paper label under base)

Left:

10-1/2" Nagpada Neighborhood House Bombay, India 1960s

Pressed cloth head, painted features, black wool hair, unjointed cloth body, stitched fingers

MADE BY POOR WOMEN AND WIDOWS, AT NAGPADA NEIGHBORHOOD HOUSE, BYCULLA, BOMBAY, INDIA, (side 1, paper tag) MARWARI LADY FROM RAJASTHAM, MONEY LENDER'S WIFE (side 2)

Right:

11-1/2" Attributed to Sont Nathu New Delhi, India 1960s

Pressed cloth head, painted features, black cloth sewn-on hair, unjointed cloth body, stitched fingers

HANDMADE INDIA // MAHARAJA KHILOWNA BRAND (paper tag) MAHARAJA // NO.33 // PRICE 12" // ICU NEW-DELHI // INDIA (2nd paper tag)

SOROMANI: the adopted child of the Retford Bee.
WOMEN'S AUXILIARY.
WESLEYAN METHODIST MISSIONARY SOCIETY. JUBILEE SERIES

A little girl, wearing a simply-wrapped Indian sari, holds her old (papier-mâché or china) doll, 1920s.

Java

About the Dolls

Every detail of the costumes of this wooden Indonesian pair is masterfully-carved and meticulously-painted. I'm always tempted to touch them and assure myself that the costumes are not really cloth! Yellow complexions, white makeup and static poses give them the aura of ancient Javanese gods.

Kimport introduced these dolls into their line in 1941 as a bridal trio, along with a servant holding a sun shade. In 1944, the Indonesian dolls were sold as a pair only.

Costume Description

Winged ear ornaments plus earrings, combs, bracelets, and chest piece form her jewelry; a batik upper body wrap; a lower body wrap and a long red batik waist ribbon.

On his head is a blue fez; ornaments are a chest piece, earrings, and bracelets; sword tucked into belt; decorative belt buckle and waist ribbon; red batik pants; brown, red, and cream colored lower body wrap.

Back of male doll (right) on opposite page.

8—9-1/2" Maker unknown Java, Indonesia c.1944

Carved wooden head with painted features, carved and painted hair, wooden one piece head and torso, not jointed

Not marked

Bride and groom of Java, Indonesia, early 20th century.

IRAN

13-1/2" Maker unknown Iran c.1941
Cloth head with hand-painted features, dark brown wool hair, cloth body over wire armature, elongated arms and legs
KIMPORT (cloth tag)

About the Doll

Kimport catalogs and issues of "Doll Talk" of the early 1940s spent quite a bit of editorial space discussing this doll, "Parizade of Persia." At that time, there was much difficulty in finding a nice example of a Persian doll; the Iranian (Persian) government no longer wished to present their people as wearing old-fashioned garments, as they were a very modern country. Finally, Kimport must have gotten their point across because this great doll arrived. Sighing with relief, Kimport praises her to the skies; she is "sheer Rubaiyat [of Omar Khayam]".

Elsie Krug, in her newsletter of January 1943, offers the Princess bride at $15 (a rather expensive doll at the time) and the matching male at $11.95. She, too, waxes eloquent over this doll as having "the grace of Saki of the Rubaiyat." The doll, in reality, is quite elongated to the point of silliness, and the edges of her veil are not even hemmed or finished, but...I can still see the visions of exotic Persia swirling about her that so inspired these poetic descriptions.

Costume Description

Persian lady in late 19th century style-indoor wear: Set at an angle is her small pink satin pillbox hat; jewelry, bead earrings and pearl necklace; hanging from the hat is a maroon brocade veil; satin brocade blouse; very short multi-color striped brocade skirt; jacket in green metallic brocade with extra long sleeves, lined in floral cotton; green striped brocade pants and leather slippers.

IRELAND

Aran Islands, County Donegal, Ulster Province

About the Dolls

Elsie Krug's International Doll House in Baltimore published a newsletter in the late 1930s and early '40s describing her offerings of international dolls. Her newsletter of March 1, 1941 describes Miss Violet M. Powell, the doll maker of Dublin. Miss Powell did life-sized studies of Aran Islands people for the Dublin Museum and national folk park; doll making was her next step.

Both Krug's company and Kimport list Violet Powell's dolls for sale in the 1940s, including a 12" praying girl, a pair of 12" twins with carrot-red hair, 10" Shaumeen the Story Teller, a 9" fisherman and old woman knitting, an 8" "keener" (ritual wailer at funerals), an 8" girl holding a doll, and others including 6" leprechauns. This doll, "Kathleen O'Flaherty" of Aran Island, has a tag from the Krug Doll House. At 15" she is the largest Violet Powell doll we have seen thus far; her sweet little 10" "daughter" is more typical of dolls you may find by Violet Powell.

Costume Description

Girl in everyday clothes: plaid kerchief; white blouse; white apron and red skirt with black band.

Woman in everyday clothes: knitted maroon sweater; black wool skirt; tweed apron and black shawl.

Irish work dress, 1910s.

10" Violet Powell Dublin, Ireland c.1940
Stockinet mask face with painted features, blonde mohair wig, cloth body with swing joints
MADE IN THE IRISH FREE STATE MADE IN SOUTHERN IRELAND
(paper tags glued onto costume)

15" Violet Powell Dublin, Ireland 1940s
Papier-mâché mask face attached to cloth head, painted features, auburn mohair wig, cloth over wire armature body
IRISH FOLK & FAIR DOLLS // VIOLET M. POWELL // SUNNYBANK // CHAPELIZOD // DUBLIN (artist's business card) MY NAME IS KATHLEEN O'FLAHERTY // AN IRISH WOMAN OF ARAN ISLAND, IRELAND // KRUG INTERNATIONAL DOLL HOUSE // 2227 ST. PAUL ST. BALTIMORE, MD (tag)
Courtesy of the Rosalie Whyel Museum of Doll Art

ITALY

Roma Province, Latium or Lazio Compartimento

About the Doll

When we find these late bisque-head dolls undressed, on simplified (sometimes crude) five piece bodies, we cannot imagine how to make them beautiful again. This pretty girl by Schoenau and Hoffmeister of Germany is an obvious reminder that clothes can make the doll! Her bright festive costume, contrasting with its virginal white headdress, transforms her!

Costume Description

White cotton TOVAGLIA (singular) on the head; metal hoop earrings, beads; white blouse, usually short puffed sleeves with frill; dark green skirt; wide bands of red and ochre yellow; an overskirt in blue-green banded in pink and tucked up in back; red velvet bodice tied at the shoulder with green bows; dark apron banded in gold braid and tied with red satin ribbon; white stockings and an elementary sandal called CIOCIE.

This costume is seen again and again in different versions, both close to reality and fanciful. It is at home in Rome and environs.

14-1/2" Schoenau & Hoffmeister Upper Franconia, Germany 1920s

Bisque socket head, inset brown glass eyes, open mouth with teeth, brown wool wig, composition five piece jointed body

S PG (IN STAR) H // 1909 // 4/0 // GERMANY

Pat Foster collection

ITALY

Roma Province, Latium or Lazio Compartimento

About the Doll

Another example of the frequently seen Italian "Roma" costume is modeled by an Italian doll made by Magis.

Many companies rather slavishly copied the beauty of Lenci, obviously hoping for Lenci's success. For companies like Magis of Rome, reasonably-priced tourist dolls were their major trade, and they did a very good job of it.

Magis dolls initially had nicely-made (albeit not as well-constructed as Lenci) cloth bodies and highly-colored felt heads. Later examples from the late 1950s onwards have plastic arms and abbreviated costumes, while attention was still lavished on the pretty faces.

Her "daughter" is a little jointed plastic doll in the same costume, with sleep eyes and molded hair. Her maker is unknown.

8-1/2" Magis Rome, Italy 1950s

Pressed felt head with painted features, black floss wig, cloth body with swing jointed limbs, stitched fingers, separate thumbs

MADE IN ITALY // MAGIS // ROMA // ROMA (gold paper tag sewn to skirt)

Young people in the costume of Roma
in Italy, c.1910.

Caserta or Sessa Arunca (just north of Naples), Napoli Province, Compania Compartimento

About the Doll

Neapolitan (Naples) wood carvers of Italy have been creating fine crèche (nativity) figures for centuries. The crèche tradition in Europe includes dozens of figures, both royalty and common folk. The villagers of early crèches from the 18th and 19th centuries are a good source for study of the folk costumes of the Naples area.

Our crèche figure is wonderfully well-preserved, despite probably being the oldest doll in this book. Her expressive face and hands with long-tapered fingers are characteristic of crèche dolls, prized for their realism. Her wig is quite unusual, as most of these dolls have carved hair.

Costume Description

Married woman's holiday dress: a small flat lace-edged headpiece which is seen throughout much of mainland Italy in a larger form; white front-tucked blouse with lace collar; black jacket, gold lace cuff trim; bodice; pleated green satin underskirt with red border and facing; pleated yellow outer skirt with red facing tucked up to show underskirt. The under-apron is red with a yellow border, the over-apron blue with a red border. Neither skirt is pleated under the two aprons.

12-1/2" Maker unknown Naples, Italy c.1800-1850

Gesso over wood shoulder head, inset brown glass eyes, open/closed mouth, black human hair wig, gesso over wood body with unjointed arms and legs

Not marked

Dorothy McGonagle collection
Photograph by Dorothy McGonagle.

ITALY

Piana dei Greci, Sicily Compartimento

12-1/2" Alberani Vecchiotti Milan, Italy c.1930s-1940s

Pressed felt head, painted features — heavy eye shadow, side-glancing eyes, black mohair wig, cloth torso and unjointed legs, swing-jointed felt arms, thumbs and 1st fingers are separate

ALBERANI // VECCHIOTTI // MILANO (gold paper wrist tag)
SICILIA // COSTUME // FESTIVO // ART. 33/20 (white paper wrist tag)

About the Doll

The authors have seen several examples of dolls by Vecchiotti; they are all of quite high quality — almost comparable to Lenci. Their faces are quite dramatic, with heavy eye shadow and high coloration; their bodies with unjointed legs are not as well-made. Felt and satin clothing is complete and quite accurate. The dolls are well-marked with a gold paper tag bearing the name of Vecchiotti and a white paper tag telling the location of the costume.

Costume Description

Woman's gala dress: hair pulled back into a chignon; blue taffeta head covering lined in pink, and painted with gold foliate designs imitating embroidery; gold necklaces and earrings; white lace edged blouse and neckerchief; red felt skirt; blue felt jacket; black net apron; ribbon tie and black felt shoes with ribbon bows.

ITALY

Val Gardena valley (northeast Italy), Venezia Tridentia Compartimento

About the Doll

Dolls by the firm of Enrico Scavini — called "Lenci" after Madame Scavini's pet name, are famous for their quality, high level of craftsmanship and appeal. A good portion of Lenci dolls were dressed in folk costumes, both Italian and many other countries. Their dolls came in a variety of sizes, from this small size called "mascotte" to the quite large, boudoir type and other specialty dolls. The small felt-faced Lenci dolls are still reasonably-priced (at least compared to the larger child dolls); a nice collection of little Lencis in Italian folk costume can still be assembled without a second mortgage.

Costume Description

Festive summer dress of young person: hair in braided chignon, bow attached; black velvet pad on head; yellow felt cylindrical hat decorated with gold metallic braid and a profusion of flowers; lace trimmed white blouse; gathered felt skirt; pink velvet bodice with green and pink trim; lacy white apron with lace edge and purple felt shoes. This falls into the Alpine style of costume.

9" Lenci (Enrico Scavini) Turin, Italy 1940s
Pressed felt swivel head with attached ears, painted side-glancing eyes, black mohair wig in braided and coiled bun, cloth body with swing-jointed arms, disc-jointed lower legs
LENCI // TORINO // MADE IN ITALY (gold tag on back of dress) VAL GARDENA (paper tag on back of dress)

JAMAICA

Left:

14" Maker unknown (possibly Pedigree) England 1950s

Plastic socket head, brown glass flirty eyes, black synthetic wig, plastic body, jointed at shoulders and hips

Not marked

Right:

14" Maker unknown Jamaica 1950s

Cloth head with painted features, black yarn wig, cloth body with swing-jointed arms and legs

JAMAICA B.W.I. (written on waistband of dress)

About the Dolls

The Jamaican boy, a handsome black doll with flirty glass eyes, was lucky indeed to be preserved in a collection of other international dolls. His Jamaican clothing, not much in quality or style, was left intact and he wasn't dressed in "nicer" clothes (an act which many of us doll collectors may be guilty!). He was no doubt made in England (Jamaica was then an English commonwealth), and dressed on-island.

His cloth companion, rocking away in the warm sun, is an "early" (1950s or '60s) example of a type of cloth doll scattered over much of the Caribbean. There is a good chance that they have all been made by the same little factory in the same country! The fabrics and styles of these dolls are much alike from country to country; they can be told apart usually only if the name of their island country is handily written on the garment.

Our Jamaican woman shows some deftness of facial painting by her artist, who bothered to show a smiling mouth with teeth. This gives her much more appeal than usual; these Caribbean cloth dolls are often very crude and cheap-looking. Look around for the earlier ones; they are usually well worth collecting.

Costume Description

His yellow print hat and shirt match; red sash; printed pants. The fabrics and prints will vary, and he may have a straw hat instead.

Her outfit includes a print head kerchief topped with a basket containing produce; gold hoop earrings; a print blouse and skirt which could also be a dress; white pinner (pinned-on) apron. Colors and prints may be different.

JAPAN

About the Doll

Artists for the last two centuries have been both fascinated and influenced by the exquisite beauty of Japanese art. An influx of Japanese prints into Europe during the last quarter of the 19th century had a major effect on artists. The work of the French Impressionists, from Manet to Degas, would not have been the same without this Japanese inspiration.

French doll makers of this late 19th century period felt much the same awe and respect for Japanese *objets d'art*. The finest and best of French doll makers, including Emile Jumeau and Leon Casimir Bru, created lovely special examples of their dolls in artful Japanese-style dress. Some of the dolls had specially-cut eyes to emulate the oriental shape; complexions were given an amber tint from subtle to quite exaggerated. They wore beautifully embroidered silk kimonos, and this example by Bru has her original fan-shaped earrings and hair ornaments.

Costume Description

Hair resembling the Japanese manner; a pale green kimono embroidered with flowers; yellow OBI sash, and fan shaped earrings. The kimono is not cut in the Japanese style of squares and rectangles. The attempt of the makers relates more closely to masquerade or fancy dress of the late 19th century.

20" Bru Jne. et Cie. Paris, France c.1885

Bisque swivel head on shoulder plate, brown glass paperweight eyes, black human hair wig, kid leather gusset-jointed body with bisque lower arms and wooden lower legs

BRU JNE 7 (head) 7 (right shoulder)
BRU JNE (left shoulder) BEBE BRU
(paper label on body)

Courtesy of the Rosalie Whyel Museum of Doll Art

JAPAN

About the Doll

This fine example of a typical modern Japanese geisha doll was purchased in Tokyo about 1986. The first floor of the doll store in Tokyo was lined with glass cases and beautifully-made dolls of all sizes and price ranges. I purchased two dolls, this one for myself and a baby doll for a friend. One of the store's proprietors, who spoke a little English, proudly explained that my doll represented one of the first geishas of Japan. When I asked if the baby doll had a special name, too, he smiled and said "ningyo" (which means "baby doll")! I was rewarded for my interest with a visit to the upstairs section of this store, which makes and sells exquisite silk kimonos.

19" Maker unknown Tokyo, Japan c.1985
Gofun (ground oyster shell) over wood shoulder head, inset black glass eyes, black human hair wig, cloth body with unjointed gofun over wood lower limbs
(Translation) JET BOY "MORNING FOG"
FINEST SILK CLOTH
LOVELY YOUNG // WOMAN

Costume Description

A top ranking courtesan of the Edo Period, most likely AGEMAKI in a KABUKI play.

Her wig with the numerous hair pins — at least twelve, and the gold cord in back tied in a specific knot, indicate AGEMAKI. The undermost kimono is white with red lining, next a rust and white kimono followed by the blue brocade jacket, UCHIKAKE (singular). Her many layered OBI (sash) is tied in front, a sign of the courtesan; wives and mothers tied the OBI in back. The white TABI (socks) are painted on this doll. The bundle of white paper at her breast is used on stage for various purposes. Keep in mind that the female roles in KABUKI are, by tradition, played by males.

Japanese courtesan-style headdress.

JAPAN

25" Maker unknown Japan c.1860

Gofun (ground oyster shell) over wood swivel head, black glass eyes, black human hair wig, gofun over wood body/legs/lower arms—dowel-jointed at hips/knees/ankles, cloth over wire upper arms

Not marked

Costume Description

Geisha from the mid-19th century: She wears the elaborate wig associated with Japan; a red under-kimono; a grey floral patterned exterior kimono and a red OBI (sash) tied with end falling down in front.

Geishas of Japan in training, holding a typical doll, c.1905.

JAPAN

About the Dolls (see pages 84-85)

The earliest of the "ichimatsu", or naturalistic play dolls, of Japan were called "mitsu-ore ningyo" (triple-jointed dolls). These Edo period (1603-1868) dolls had adult faces and were jointed with wooden pins at the hip, knee and ankle. They often had elaborate clothes, even wardrobes or changeable wigs. Jill and David Gribben, in their beautiful book entitled *Japanese Antique Dolls*, discuss these dolls in detail and note the fact that many of the triple-jointed dolls were owned by adult women, not children. A superb example of these early dolls is shown on the opposite page.

Later examples of the "ichimatsu" dolls have joints linked together with silk or paper, sometimes also with a covered space at the waist containing a squeaker. The faces became more childlike, even babyish. The construction of these "baby" dolls heavily influenced makers of Western-style dolls in Germany and France.

Toward the end of the Meiji era (1868-1912) the type of doll that the Gribbens call the "display ichimatsu" came into popularity. These were not really for play anymore, and often kept in glass cases. Some specialists of Japanese dolls call these "Yamato-ningyo"; "Yamato" is the ancient name of Japan.

Our fine example of the later "ichimatsu" (or "Yamato-ningyo") doll is a cherished one, purchased in Tokyo in 1936 for a Seattle-born Japanese girl by her mother. The doll was preserved in a homemade cardboard "case" and is in pristine condition, as bright and beautiful as the day she was given as a gift of heritage.

Costume Description

Young girl: short hair with bangs; red under-kimono; over that another white under-kimono, followed by a bright multicolor outer-kimono and red brocade OBI (sash). Bright colors are worn by children and young people, red being popular. Older people wear smaller prints and calm color combinations.

Young woman in ordinary dress holding "ichimatsu" type doll, Japan, early 20th century.

15-1/2" Maker unknown Japan 1936

Gofun (ground oyster shell) over wood head, inset black glass eyes, black human hair wig, cloth- and paper-wrapped cardboard and gofun over wood body, cloth joints between body and limbs

Not marked

Courtesy of the Rosalie Whyel Museum of Doll Art

Country costume

About the Doll

Even the smallest of Japanese dolls, made as inexpensive tourist pieces, is often well-crafted and quite detailed. This pride of craftsmanship translates into so many of their dolls. This small doll (7") in country costume could have easily been made in plastic, with a much simpler costume and painted details like the sandals. Instead she wears a multiple-layered costume, headdress and separate sandals.

Costume Description

Country woman: white head kerchief with blue and white back; a red, then a white under-kimono; a blue and white IKAT outer-kimono; red and white OBI (sash); white TABI (socks) with ZORI (sandals). Wood faggots on her head.

7" Maker unknown Japan 1960s

Painted composition head, inset black glass eyes, black human hair wig, cardboard body with unjointed limbs, painted composition hands and feet.

Not marked

Courtesy of the Rosalie Whyel Museum of Doll Art

Japanese cotton resist fabric.

Ramallah, Judean Hills

About the Dolls

Thanks to a cloth tag on the dolls' costumes listing their maker — the Arab Refugee Handworks Centre in Jerusalem, Jordan — we know that this pair of dolls was personally crafted by Miss A. G. Malaby. She was probably the person who painted the lively faces on flat, oval cloth backgrounds. The bodies are much simpler cloth (albeit satin!) over wire affairs. Their garments are wonderful miniature replicas of the adult costume from Ramallah shown here, in the collection of the Rosalie Whyel Museum of Doll Art. The intricate embroidery of the yokes of our dolls' robes is all done by hand.

Costume Description

Best dresses: white for summer and dark blue for winter. Long veil worn over a head roll of sequins instead of coins; long open sleeved embroidered dress; sash of striped material or gold braid. There can be an underdress and also long pantaloons. The cross-stitch embroidery will depict geometric plants, flowers, and trees.

Woman's embroidered dress from Ramallah, Jordan, early 20th century. *Courtesy of the Rosalie Whyel Museum of Doll Art.*

14-1/2" Miss A.G. Malaby (Arab Refugee Handworks Centre) Jerusalem, Jordan c.1940
Cloth head with painted features, black wool wisps of hair, cloth body over wire armature
MADE BY THE ARAB REFUGEE // HANDWORKS CENTRE // IN JERUSALEM, JORDAN // MISS A.G. MALABY

Masai people
(also live in northern Tanzania)

About the Doll

The Masai warrior is carved of one piece of wood, his elongated body representing the tall figure and long neck desirable among Masai men. The shape of the wood used for these dolls determines their final shape. The garment here is of very little consequence; rather, it is the carving of the head, elaborate hairstyle and beadwork that make it a classic "primitive" work.

Costume Description

This hair arrangement distinguishes the Masai warrior. Triangular bead earrings, necklace, ankle rings. Cotton or hide wrap garment. Man may carry sword and shield. A real shield would be of buffalo hide.

Women have many more neck and ankle rings than the men, otherwise the attire appears much the same.

11" Maker unknown Kenya 1970s

Wooden head with carved features and white bead eyes, carved hair, unjointed wood body

Not marked

Meo (Miao) or H'Moong (Mong) people

About the Doll

Present day Laos is part of what was once called French Indo China, which also included Vietnam and Cambodia. French-made celluloid dolls in local dress can be found from this period, and Kimport discovered a source for the delicate cloth doll shown here. In 1939 Kimport illustrated a male version, whom they named "Seng Lun," his face "painted in oils by an artist of the mission on the Mekong River." An information sheet which was sent with each doll shows the same catalog illustration, but calls him "Sing Ming;" it also alludes to a lady friend named "Supi Lun" who I assume is our doll.

Today it is difficult to find any quality dolls from the nations that once formed Indo China; so I continue to search for lovely older examples like this one.

Costume Description

She displays a navy blue turban; white pompons in back; silver earrings, bracelets and torque (open necklace); white blouse with collar; white pleated skirt embroidered in blue, red, and green; a hip length blue jacket embroidered and braided in red, white, and blue; plain oblong blue apron; wide blue cotton belt with blue, red, and white embroidery; black slippers.

9-3/4" Maker unknown Laos (formerly French Indo China) c.1940

Cloth head, hand-painted features, painted black hair, cloth body with swing-jointed limbs, stitched fingers

Made in // French Indochina (paper tag)
KIMPORT (cloth tag)

Dance group in dress of the Meo people, Southeast Asia, 1960s.

Nica, Kurzeme Province

12" Maker unknown (Doll — "Tammy" by Ideal) United States (Dressed by a Latvian American) 1960s

Vinyl swivel head, painted features, light brown synthetic hair, vinyl body with jointed arms and legs

IDEAL TOY CORP. // BS-12

About the Doll

The Latvian doll is typical of plastic dolls purchased undressed and clothed in folk costumes by immigrants to the United States. Our Latvian doll, for instance, is a "Tammy" doll made by Ideal. This type of doll is sold to raise money for ethnic groups at museums, bazaars, and other celebrations. The quality of the dolls themselves is often only fair but the costumes can be quite elaborate and authentic.

Costume Description

Stiffened red wool crown with silver braid, pearls and beads; long sleeved white blouse; red embroidery at shoulder and collar; large round metal pins at neck and waist represent sun symbols; bodice with peplum in grey felt with dark machine stitching; gathered red wool skirt embroidered in white and green. Skirt may have border of yellow and blue. May also have a large homespun wool shawl with bright embroidery, worn around the body and pinned at the shoulder.

LESOTHO

7-1/2"—8" Lesotho Cooperative Handicrafts Lesotho, Africa 1980s

Cloth head with white sequin eyes and felt mouth, no hair, unjointed cloth body

Not marked

About the Dolls

There are no marks or tags on these quaint brown cloth dolls but Loretta Holz identified them as being made by the Lesotho Cooperative Handicrafts organization. Later research found the dolls in a 1980s catalog from SERVV (SERVV is a self-help company which distributes handicrafts from various third-world countries). Mail order catalogs for agencies like these, plus other import companies in business today, are a good source for handmade dolls in folk costume. On occasion, a maker or cooperative's name will even be listed (save this page, as the information will often not be on the doll).

Lesotho is a tiny, land-locked country within the larger nation of South Africa. These little dolls reflect the peoples' love for wearing their colorful, handmade blankets and conical woven hats. The dolls are simply-made but charming.

Costume Description

Modern daily wear: both wear straw hats with a top loop; colored blanket wrap banded in black, fastened with a decorative safety pin. Man with khaki pants and shirt; woman in blue and white dress.

MACEDONIA

About the Doll

Our maiden from Macedonia is both the earliest and the largest doll we have seen by the Near East Industries, a division of the Near East Foundation of New York. Maria Argyriadi, in her book on Greek dolls, reports that in 1922 the Near East Foundation had two branches, one in Athens and the other in Macedonia. "Work centers" were set up to assist refugees from Asia Minor and the Balkans, and dolls and other salable items were produced to raise money. Kimport had a contract with the Near East Foundation, but the dolls they imported were exclusively the later, much smaller dolls represented in this book elsewhere (see Greece and Albania).

This doll's face was almost completely washed away when we found her. She has been painstakingly restored, using shadows of original lines and pictures from Maria Argyriadi's book, by artist and doll restorer Joan Bergstrom.

Costume Description

A white embroidered kerchief (here missing) worn over a red cap; white embroidered chemise; off-white sleeveless coat banded in red; red sash having ornamental stitching and fringes; red wool apron trimmed with gold rick-rack; black striped stockings and black shoes.

This doll came with information indicating it was Greek Macedonian. Despite the rather detailed information included with the doll, the conclusion is that it is of Macedonia (former Yugoslavia) and has elements of Mariova, the Struga-Ohrid area and the area south of Debar.

17" Near East Industries Athens, Greece 1920s-1930s

Pressed cloth head, painted features, brown mohair wig in four braids, muslin body with disc-jointed cloth limbs, stitched fingers, separate thumbs

NEAR EAST // INDUSTRIES // SPONSORED AND SUPERVISED BY THE // NEAR EAST FOUNDATION // 151 FIFTH AVENUE NEW YORK (paper tag on back of costume) #15 // MACEDONIA (inscribed in pencil on back of tag)

Paper tag shows information on the maker, Near East Industries.

Overseas Department of France

About the Doll

Martinique was a French possession from 1635 until 1946, when it was granted some autonomy. Many of the dolls dressed in the beautiful native costumes have been of French manufacture. Wonderful papier-mâché dolls from the 19th century exist from Martinique, plus early 20th century bisque head dolls by S.F.B.J., and finally these lovely-complexioned celluloids from the mid-20th century made by celebrated factories like Petitcollin and Société Nobel Française. A number of these latter-day celluloids, quality dolls of various sizes, are found marked with "Sandra Dogue" wrist tags.

Costume Description

This doll has a plaid turban with three points; a green crepe paper hair bow; silver earrings and necklaces; cream color lace off-the-shoulder blouse; rich yellow brocade

gathered skirt; a red shoulder kerchief worn from shoulder to opposite hip; a visible ecru lace petticoat and black shoes.

Martinique became a French colony in 1635. This costume reflects colonial dress. The Empress Josephine was born here and her house is now a museum.

16" Les Poupées Sandra Dogue (celluloid doll by Petitcollin) France c.1950s
Celluloid socket head, brown glass inset eyes with mohair eyelashes, painted mouth and beauty mark, brown mohair wig coiled over paper frame, celluloid body with jointed arms and legs.
(EAGLE MARK) // FRANCE // 36 (body)

TYPE DE MULATRESSE DE SAINT-PIERRE DE LA MARTINIQUE

Girl from Martinique in a slightly different headpiece, 1907.

MEXICO

(Male) Charro, (Female) China Poblana

About the Dolls

Nice quality composition dolls, far better than the usual souvenir dolls out of Mexico. Both dolls are well-made and have dramatic, glamorous looks no doubt inspired by popular Hollywood movies. Lovely, dark-eyed Latina women like Rita Hayworth and Carmen Miranda were popular movie stars; and, of course, there was debonair Desi Arnaz. The effect of this ideal Hispanic beauty influenced dolls, even ones from Latin American countries themselves.

The dolls' clothing is well-detailed; it offers a nice contrast of a sharply-tailored black and white suit to the billowy, colorful skirts and sparkly sombreros.

Costume Description

The CHARRO suit evolved from Spanish prototypes and is worn by the hacienda cowboys and members of Sunday riding clubs. His outfit has a large sombrero; white cotton shirt; red tie; black jacket and pants trimmed in white cord, and a multicolored serape.

Legend attributes various origins to the CHINA costume and its use in the city of Puebla. She has a sombrero; a white blouse which may be embroidered or beaded; red skirt with green top, sequins sprinkled over all; petticoat customarily protrudes below the skirt; a sash at the waist and a REBOZO (multipurpose stole). Although these costumes are called the national costumes of Mexico, both are post conquest developments.

11" Maker unknown Mexico c.1949

Composition head with painted features, painted brown hair (Male) Black floss hair (Female), cloth body with jointed composition arms and legs

Not marked

Courtesy of the Rosalie Whyel Museum of Doll Art

Group of Mexican *charros* and *chinas*, c.1920s.

Lake Pátzcuaro District, State of Michoácan

About the Doll

The Michoácan doll presents a striking contrast — country to town and everyday drab to festive glamour — to the Mexican china poblana and charro. The sturdy and chunky peasant woman certainly would have no home in a Hollywood movie, but she relieves her somber daily clothing with bright bits of embroidery and trim, and a large and useful fringed REBOZO thrown over her shoulder.

She is not strictly a doll, not in the classic sense of a movable human figure. But with dolls in costume, collectors must often make exceptions, enabling them to acquire beautiful objects that blur the line between dolls and sculptures. The Michoácan woman is a very monumental and striking figure, from her four-square face to the simple but beautifully-carved braid down her back.

Costume Description

Hair in one long braid; embroidery painted on white square necked HUIPIL (singular) or blouse; dark blue wool pleated skirt tied with woven belt;

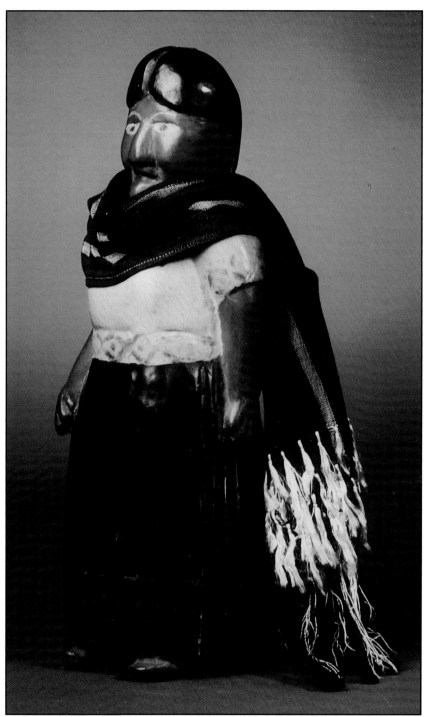

navy blue apron with painted lower edge; a woven fabric REBOZO (stole). This skirt is formed of hand-woven lengths of fabric sewn to form a tube and then pleated with each wearing onto the body. Many belts may be used to hold the skirt.

11" Maker unknown Mexico c.1950s
Painted wooden head with painted features, carved hair in braid down back, unjointed wooden body
P 53 E3 12.00 (written on base)

Isthmus of Tehuantepec

About the Doll

A type of cloth Mexican doll that is found in a variety of regional costumes (both male and female), and dates from the late 1930s and 1940s. Travel to Mexico by Americans and other tourists was on a dramatic rise during this period, and many dolls can be found, ranging from quite interesting (like these) to crude and cheap. Mexican themes and colors invaded American households — witness the popularity of Fiestaware dishes and of Mexican embroidered skirts and blouses.

A doll collector who took apart a doll like this one in poor condition, discovered a creative recycling of materials. The glass-like eyes were made of small dried beans with the pupils painted on. The open mouth is full of teeth that are actually white seed beads. Rough homespun cloth is used for the bodies and pressed-mask faces.

These are very distinctive dolls that, once accustomed to them, you will recognize immediately. I have seen a number of other examples in the last several years; Johana Anderton shows a couple with a baby from about 1941 in her *Encyclopedia of Cloth Dolls* (p. 234). No record of their maker has yet been found.

One of several ways to wear the headdress of Tehuantepec in Mexico, 1941.

Costume Description

Festive attire: Three garments are the total of this elegant costume. A short unfitted blouse called HUIPIL GRANDE (singular); a gathered skirt with wide lace flounce. Both garments embroidered on satin. The headdress called HUIPIL CHICO (singular) looks very like a baby dress. Several stories account for this similarity, one having to do with priests' vestments and shipwrecks, another with baby clothes. A large gold coin necklace, part of her dowry, is worn. She wears the HUIPIL CHICO according to the social or religious function she is attending.

11" Maker unknown Mexico 1940s-1950s
Pressed cloth head, inset bean eyes with painted pupils, open mouth with white bead teeth, black yarn hair, cloth body, not jointed
Not marked
Courtesy of the Rosalie Whyel Museum of Doll Art

MOROCCO

(Female) Berber people, Gorge Du Dades; (Male) Sahara— Tuareg people

About the Dolls

Tuaregs and Berbers are fiercely independent Bedouin peoples of northern Africa. The Tuareg men, with their blue face coverings against the sand and sun, are known as the Blue Men. Berber women often wear outlandish clothing, the brilliant colors and textures of their desert-wear clash and jar to western eyes.

Both recently made by the company La Mode, the dolls are as colorful as the people they personify. The Tuareg wears his light blue caftan and dark blue face; a note inside his wrist tag tells that the "Blue Man" is the wanderer of the Sahara Desert. His Berber companion has a rather garish blouse and hat; a fire engine red silk scarf was unraveled to form her hair. A white lacy skirt and pink leather slippers (which stay on her stubby feet only with some difficulty) created by the famous leather artisans of Morocco, complete her vibrant ensemble.

Costume Description

Woman wearing a turban in multicolored brocade and fringe, tied with a black ornamental band; green multicolored open sleeved dress; over robe of black and gold lace with split sides and open front; over skirt of white and gold lace; black cord belt ending in bright tassels, and embroidered pink slippers. Underneath are blue printed pantaloons.

Man in black cotton turban and face veil called the LITHAM; wide white pants; white closed long robe; pale blue striped over robe with yellow machine embroidery at neck and on pocket.

11—12-1/2" La Mode Morocco 1993

Cloth head, half sequin eyes with thread across to depict pupils, embroidered mouth, no hair (Male), red silk fringe wig (Female), unjointed cloth body

HANDCRAFTED IN MOROCCO // LA MODE DOLLS (paper tag on female)

MOROCCO

About the Dolls

Two versions of the old water carriers, thirty or forty years apart in their crafting, meet in the streets of Morocco. The postcard shows us how accurately the dolls depict this once very crucial occupation. With a goatskin bag of water, a variety of metal drinking vessels and a bell to announce his arrival, the molded-leather doll on the right was sold to tourists and imported into the United States by Kimport, Velvalee Dickinson, and probably others in the 1930s and '40s. Moroccan leather artisans were known the world over.

The later doll is no longer of leather due to its expense, but still cleverly crafted, this time by wrapping thread around and around a wire armature. He stops his elderly companion here for advice and interesting conversation.

Costume Description

Water seller working outfit: one man wearing a head wrap and the other a cap; one a striped tunic and the other a shirt and tunic; knee pants; sandals. Both carry skin bags for water and metal cups for serving.

Water vendor in the streets of Marrakech, Morocco, 1930s.

6. MAROC. — Le marchand d'eau.

Left:

10-1/2" Maker unknown Morocco 1950s-1960s

Thread-wrapped molded swivel head, painted features, painted black hair, thread-wrapped wire armature body

Not marked

- -

Right:

11" Maker unknown Morocco c.1939

Molded leather head, molded and painted features, brown wool over painted brown hair, cloth torso with swing-jointed leather arms, unjointed leather legs

Not marked

NETHERLANDS
Marken, Noord Holland Province

About the Dolls

Armand Marseille, German doll maker with a prodigious output, shipped dolls or in some cases only the bisque heads to various parts of the globe to be made into souvenirs for tourists. Other examples can be seen in this book under Norway and Croatia, but there are many different costumes found on their dolls.

Armand Marseille may have made these Marken dolls for Gerzon, an importer and distributor of dolls in the Netherlands, who in 1928 advertised 24cm (about 9") dolls in regional costumes of Marken, Volendam, and Goes (see the Coleman's *Encyclopedia of Dolls, Vol. II*).

Often dressed by small cottage industry workers in their homes, the souvenir dolls were made to sell to an increasingly mobile world of tourists. This delightful pair of Armand Marseille dolls from the little island of Marken (now connected to the mainland by a causeway) have very accurate local costumes created from authentic fabrics — compare them to the actual child's costume. They are detailed enough to capture the quaint Marken custom of a single long sausage curl on either side of the head for both girls and young boys. The postcard shows this costume, with both the younger boy in pants on the right, and the slightly older boy on the left who is shorn of his curls.

Costume Description

Young boy: from the waist up, the boy's costume is very like the girl's until age six or seven. White knitted lace cap over red; hair has two corkscrew curls hanging in front. Floral print under garment except for plaid plastron decorated with lace and pinned at the neck; full black cotton knee pants (a male garment); black stockings and wooden shoes.

Young girl: white knitted lace cap over red; hair flows down back with two corkscrew curls in front; floral print blouse, cuffs of red and white braid; different floral print plastron over the blouse; navy blue sateen skirt pleated into waistband of dark red wool braid. The skirt is not pleated under the apron, a practice found over much of Europe. Navy blue cotton apron with red and white checked top; black stockings and wooden shoes. She changes her costume also at age six or seven.

Marken boys and girls, Netherlands, c.1920s.

Mid 20th century girl's costume and cap from Marken, Netherlands.

8-1/2" Maker unknown (doll by Armand Marseille, Koppelsdorf, Germany) (costuming) Marken, Netherlands 1920s

Bisque socket head, blue glass sleep eyes, open mouth, brown mohair wig, jointed five piece composition body

ARMAND MARSEILLE // GERMANY // 390 // A 12/OX M

*Photograph of dolls appears on page 100.

Marken boy and girl by Armand Marseille. *See page 99.*

NETHERLANDS
Volendam, Noord Holland Province

About the Dolls

The Havik Doll Shop lies in the middle of the heavily-tourristed village of Volendam, whence comes the best-known costume of Holland.

In her limited English, the proprietor of the Havik shop told me that she and her husband "made" the wooden doll on the left, which I assume meant that they assembled and dressed her. They insisted the same thing about a pair of dolls with bisque heads; the dolls were obviously newly-made in Taiwan and dressed by the Havik shop in Volendam costume.

The little Volendam girl's beautifully-carved head, arms and legs are virtually the same as the Italian dolls by Dolfi, advertised heavily in the late 1980s. The doll or her wooden parts were probably purchased from Italy by the Havik Company and dressed, creating a very unusual type of doll from Volendam. She was purchased in 1994.

Her little brother is another bisque-head doll by Armand Marseille, this time a character boy, mold #560. He personifies the classic, round-cheeked little Dutch child with wooden shoes that we remember from books, postcards, valentines, and even kitchen cleanser.

Costume Description

Female festive attire: lace cap with turned-back wings, hair would be tucked under cap and should be tied in back; red-orange plastic necklace imitating coral; black wool over-blouse, trim of green satin ribbon and black and white braid; gathered striped flannelette skirt in primary colors; gathered black wool apron with black and white braid; top of apron in floral print with matching dickey; black stockings and wooden shoes, so associated with the Lowlands. Several petticoats are worn and earlier a padded hip roll or bolster called a BUM ROLL was worn, creating a full silhouette. We see its origins in the 16th and 17th centuries. This costume is one of the most commonly depicted to represent the Netherlands on dolls and in travel brochures.

Male festive attire: black velvet hat, bow on side; red shirt with band collar; red and black striped jacket with large buttons; wide black sateen pants with large red buttons; black stockings and wooden shoes. There are striped underpants following the shape of the outer pants.

Above Left: 12" Havik Dolls Volendam, Netherlands (Wood parts probably from Italy) 1994

Carved wooden flange head, painted features, brown synthetic wig, cloth body with wooden hands and lower legs

CERTIFICATE HAVIK DOLLS // VOLENDAM-HOLLAND // SINCE 1880. DOLLS & CLOTHES HANDMADE IN OUR FAMILY (paper wrist tag)

Above Right: 11" Armand Marseille Koppelsdorf, Germany c.1920

Bisque socket head, painted eyes, open/closed mouth, molded hair, jointed five piece papier-mâché body

560 // GERMANY // A 3/0 M DRGM

Pat Foster collection

Dovina celluloid dolls in Dutch costume of Volendam, 1950s.

NETHERLANDS

Spakenberg village, Utrecht Province

About the Doll

The Dovina Company of Rotterdam dressed celluloid and, more recently, plastic and vinyl dolls in the various regional costumes of the Netherlands. The dolls themselves are not marked, but a cloth identifying tag is well-sewn onto the back of their garments.

The earliest Dovina dolls we have found are from about 1950; the company was still offering dolls in the mid-1970s, but has subsequently apparently closed. A trip through Holland in 1994 found none of these dolls for sale.

Our young lady was purchased in 1969; dig her 1960s pop-art fabric petticoat!

Costume Description

Adult costume: The over cap is white crochet with a black under cap. Earlier there was a third fine lace cap over these two. Hair cut short in back, and the front hair rolled up in front of the caps. Black wool blouse with separate red plaid lower sleeve and a unique winged floral garment called a KRAPLAP (singular) which is tied with strings and rolls over the shoulders to the back. Over this is a red diagonal plaid tie which is in front and back; dark blue apron with plaid top; black stockings and wooden shoes; black and white print petticoat. Nowadays, black shoes are more normal.

Spakenburg residents in everyday attire, Netherlands, early 20th century.

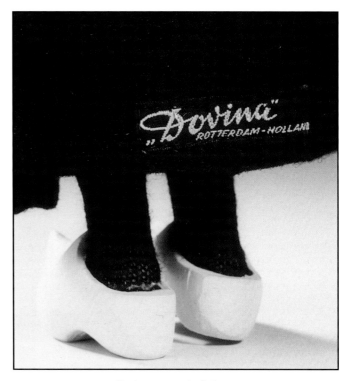

Dovina company's cloth tag.

9" Dovina Rotterdam, Netherlands 1969
Plastic head with painted features, brown synthetic wig, plastic body with jointed arms and legs
DOVINA ROTTERDAM - HOLLAND (cloth tag on back of skirt)

Zuid-Beveland Area, Zeeland Province

About the Doll

Like the little girls holding their rag doll in the postcard, this unusual and lovely character doll is from the Zeeland region of Holland. The serene, slightly-smiling face of this rare mold #1478 by master German porcelain factory Simon and Halbig is framed by her starched white head kerchief. She wears a pair of rectangular brass ornaments (these can also be corkscrew-shaped) attached to a half-circular headpiece under cap; in real life these ornaments were often made of gold.

Costume Description

Woman wearing a white lace edged cap over a metal base supporting disks on each side; red bead necklace imitating coral, which is considered lucky; black wool bodice-with-sleeves; plastron of purple and white stripes; blue and white yoke; pastel neckerchief gathered at the shoulders; black gathered wool skirt; navy blue cotton apron; black stockings and wooden shoes called KLOMPEN.

The disks to the side of the head are round for Catholics and square for Protestants.

15" Simon and Halbig Grafenhain, Germany c.1913
Bisque socket head, brown glass sleep eyes, closed mouth, brown mohair wig, ball-jointed composition body
1478 // S & H // 5
Courtesy of the Rosalie Whyel Museum of Doll Art

Zeeland girls playing with their rag doll, Netherlands, early 20th century.

Maori people

About the Doll

A most interesting Maori girl, made from a heavy pottery and well-marked as to maker — Lang's of Wellington, New Zealand. Considering that some of the other Maori dolls we have found are plastic and sometimes charmless, this girl was a great find. Her construction is quite simple; in fact, she appears to have been cast in a mold made from an existing doll and coated with a very thick paint. She is dressed very simply but accurately with natural materials.

Costume Description

Hair in two braids, red ties; black and white braided headband; green plastic TIKI (image of a god) tied to her shawl; red cotton wrap top; grass skirt; beige cotton shoulder wrap with hanging black wool strings.

11-1/2" Langs Wellington, New Zealand c.1940s
Ceramic socket head with painted features, black wool hair, ceramic body with jointed arms and legs
LANGS // WELLINGTON // NZ P

A view of Maori women in native textiles, New Zealand, c.1910s.

Hausa people

About the Dolls

Despite the effort by S.F.B.J., the French doll and toy conglomerate of the early 20th century, to create lesser-priced dolls to compete successfully with German ones, they also kept alive some of the grand French doll traditions. One of these traditions was doll costuming.

French fashions led the western world and the frilly fashion world of dolls was no exception. Victorian high-style for children (of means) was elegantly reflected in French bébés or child dolls.

French doll makers always loved to show off their fine work at world fairs and exhibitions. At times, their dolls got the exotic treatment, being dressed to the nines in the colorful garb of faraway French possessions in the West Indies or in mysterious Africa. An early example of one of these exotics is the fabulous Bru lady from Senegal, shown on page 132. From the S.F.B.J. period is this incredible pair of character-style dolls, black versions of the #227 mold, depicting the Hausa people of Nigeria.

Layers of vibrant clothing, tangled necklaces of leather pouches — each containing a special Moslem prayer — her myriad "mud-caked" (black string) braids, and the vitality and charm of their joyous faces, are all details to be savored and enjoyed. French dolls...reflecting their glorious past!

Costume Description

The Hausa people are itinerant merchants who roam much of West Africa.

Wrapped on her head is a yellow silk turban; leather necklaces like the man's; a white under robe; a pale green brocade over robe; a striped wrap skirt and, underneath that, three more under skirts.

On his head is a soft purple velvet hat embroidered with the star and crescent in gold; five leather necklaces consisting of small pouches which would contain Muslim prayers and quotations from the Koran; a white striped and embroidered robe called a RIGA (singular); underneath a green wool coat with gold buttons and red banding; reddish-brown knee pants.

20" Société Française de Fabrication de Bébés et Jouets Paris, France c.1910s

Bisque socket head, dark brown glass inset eyes, black flocked wig (Male), black cord wig (Female), ball-jointed composition and wood body

S.F.B.J // 227 // PARIS // 8

Courtesy of the Rosalie Whyel Museum of Doll Art

Voss, Hordaland County, Hardänger Area

About the Dolls

Fine quality German china-head dolls, dressed in perhaps the best-known, and certainly the most frequently seen on dolls, Norwegian costume. The area known as Hardänger is famous for its needlework as seen, simplified, on the aprons, and in the intricate beadwork patterns on the wool bodices. I have seen several other female examples of these Hardänger china-head dolls on similar cloth bodies with dainty china hands; on occasion, they will carry a baby like this one in beaded cloth pouch. However, this is the only example of the rare male doll I have seen to date. He is as meticulously-dressed as his companion. The dolls are wonderfully well-preserved for their age (nearly 150 years old).

Costume Description (pages 106-107)

Man in soft red hat with tassel; white cotton shirt; blue vest bordered in red with red button holes, sequin buttons; white jacket bordered in red; belt with buckle; black knee pants and black buckled shoes. The costumes of Hardänger are the most often used to represent Norway.

There are other costumes of Hardänger very similar including that of Fana with a blue edged bodice. In the costume of Voss, the bodice has a narrow back and green

velvet border. It would have a wide green velvet and silver lace skirt border. A headdress with black work embroidery is also worn in Voss.

Married woman's festive dress of the 19th century: Young girls would wear a colored headband or small cap. The pleated and starched white head kerchief, SKAUT (singular), indicates a married woman. Two pins worn at neck; white linen blouse and apron with lace inserts, here replacing the famous Hardänger drawn work. Red wool bodice; beaded plastron; black wool skirt, earlier of dark blue; woven belt is in green and red and may also be beaded. A black jacket as on our second example may be worn.

12"—13" Maker unknown Germany 1860s-1870s

China shoulder head with painted features, painted black hair, cloth body with china lower arms

Not marked

Courtesy of the Rosalie Whyel Museum of Doll Art

Early plastic or celluloid dolls in Hardänger bridal dress, Norway, c.1950.

Voss, Hordaland County, Hardänger Area

About the Doll

A superb early shoulder head by Simon & Halbig with subtly-painted eyes. Her linen body is original but probably handmade, with quite elongated legs and dense stuffing, making the doll quite heavy. Her graceful bisque lower arms were probably purchased commercially at the same time as the head. Unique to this doll, her lower legs were hand-carved of wood.

Her costume is sewn from heavy, warm woolen and homespun cotton fabrics and is molded to her body as if she has lived in it for over a century. She came from a family in the Ballard area of Seattle, settled by Scandinavian people. She has a "feel" — like some untouched dolls do, of an heirloom and a treasure of the family's national heritage.

Costume Description (see page 106)

23" Simon & Halbig Grafenhain, Germany c.1880s

Bisque solid dome head on shoulder plate, painted blue eyes, closed mouth, blonde mohair wig, linen body, bisque lower arms, hand-carved wooden lower legs

S & H (front shoulder plate)

Heddal, Ost Telemark County

About the Doll

Ronnaug Petterssen, creator of splendidly-crafted felt and cloth Norwegian dolls, was born in 1901 and died in 1980. She studied art in Berlin in 1929-30, then traveled to Spain and the Balearic Islands to study folk costume and doll making. Ronnaug returned to her home in Oslo in 1934 and started a doll studio, achieving acclaim so quickly that she was asked to create an exhibit of "Norway in Dolls" for the 1937 World Exhibition in Paris. A few years later, in 1939-40, she exhibited Norwegian dolls at the New York World's Fair.

Ronnaug Petterssen's earlier dolls of felt and cloth came in sizes from 8" to 18". The smaller dolls (imported by Kimport and other companies) are made of cloth over wire armatures; the larger ones have disc-jointed cloth bodies and removable clothing. The vast majority of her dolls have painted eyes, although a rare few have been seen with inset glass eyes. Dolls with plastic heads and limbs came later, in the 1950s.

The various costumes of Norway, plus costumes of Petterssen's beloved Laplanders, were woven, embroidered and sewn by women from all over Norway. Several articles

The Norwegian "red jacket costume" of Telemark, 1940s.

have been written on this gifted doll artist; please see the bibliography for details.

Costume Description

Unmarried woman's festive wear: woven headband; white long sleeved blouse; silver pin at neck; long black skirt banded in red, blue and green; red bodice; black gathered apron with floral embroidery at the hem and part way up the side in primary colors; red woven sash tied to one side; red wool long sleeved jacket with black edging, ochre yellow lower edge, and multicolored embroidery at the neck. Not surprisingly called the "red jacket costume."

17-1/2" Ronnaug Petterssen Oslo, Norway c.1940

Pressed felt swivel head with painted blue eyes, blonde mohair wig, cloth body with swing-jointed arms and disc-jointed legs, separate thumbs

MADE IN NORWAY // (LOGO OF LAPLANDER) // VARE-MARKE (blue paper tag with gold lettering) RONNAUG PETTERSSEN (reverse of paper tag)

Sunnmore, More and Romsdal County

About the Doll

A very long-legged girl with the ubiquitous Armand Marseille mold #390 head, this time a later version with sprayed-on facial coloring. Her costume is elaborately embroidered, obviously done by hand by a needleworker trained in the creation of Norwegian costumes. Since the embroidery is quite heavy, it must have been difficult to scale this costume down to doll-size; the seamstress did an excellent job. The back of the bodice, which I wish you could also see, is entirely covered with lovely embroidery. You can see more of this splendid Norwegian embroidery in the detail below of an adult-sized belt.

Our Sunnmore girl might have been dressed as a special commission for a family; she was not likely a tourist souvenir.

Costume Description

A woman's BUNAD is a recreated costume from earlier prototypes, this one designed in 1927. The BUNAD of Valdres and the formal BUNAD of Gudbandstal are similar. This hat is somewhat thicker than the real hat called KOLLE-HAT (singular). Pin and bodice hooks here in rhinestones, reality would call for silver. White silk blouse, linen or cotton would be more usual. Black wool pleated skirt, black wool bodice and pleated apron, all three pieces embroidered in primary colors; red stockings and black shoes with buckles.

She could have an embroidered skirt-pocket. Alternate headwear is a white linen kerchief embroidered and tied on with colored silk ties.

24" Armand Marseille Koppelsdorf, Germany (costuming probably in Norway)   1930s
Painted bisque socket head, blue glass eyes and eyelashes, open mouth with teeth, blonde mohair wig, cloth torso, legs and upper arms, composition lower arms
ARMAND MARSEILLE // GERMANY // 390 // A5M

Norwegian embroidered wool belt, dated 1913.

PAKISTAN

Sindh Province

About the Doll

This is really quite a grand Pakistani doll. The simplicity of her cloth construction (similar to the dolls from India) allows her to carry off quite exotic makeup, a nose-ring, and a very elaborately embroidered, painted and mirrored costume. Compare her to the actual child's costume shown here, and you can see that the doll's tunic was probably cut down from a real one. It is not a bit less ornate!

She was purchased in 1970 from an import store in California. I have seen several other Pakistani dolls by the same maker; unfortunately, none are tagged.

Costume Description

The Sindhi woman exhibits a festive aspect. Hair in braids; red cotton hand-painted veil; earrings and beads; red cotton tunic with multicolored embroidery and mirrors; wide striped pantaloons and gold braid sandals.

12" Maker unknown Pakistan or India 1970

Pressed cloth head with hand-painted features, black floss hair, cloth body with cloth over wire arms, stitched fingers with separate thumbs

Not marked

Tunic from Pakistan, early 20th century

(Male) El Montuno costume (Female) La Pollera costume

About the Dolls

Continuing an old tradition of imported dolls costumed in the country, these Reliable of Canada dolls ended up in Panama City, where they were purchased by a tourist in 1966. Although the dolls are of a type that are still considered quite cheap by collectors, they are very attractive. The female has a lovely black mohair wig accentuated by her hair decorations. The male with his painted-on mustache looks a bit silly (as male dolls made up from female doll molds often do), but he has a jaunty woven "Panama hat" and added sandals. Kimport offered similar dolls in the early 1960s for $5 each.

Costume Description

He sports his EL MONTUNO costume of a Panama straw hat turned up in front and fastened with a bright colored pompon; a long shirt and knee pants of muslin are embroidered with bright cross-stitch birds

and animals, with leather sandals. The cut and fabric will be the same but the embroidery motifs may vary.

The lady wears LA POLLERA (singular) dress. The blouse has a very deep double flounce of embroidery and lace falling from a tight lace off-the-shoulder band decorated with bright colored pompons front and back; a full gathered embroidered skirt has a bright ribbon falling from the waist called GALLARDETE (singular); gold jewelry is worn and her hair ornaments of sequins, pearls, and silver are attached to wires so as to tremble as she moves, named TEM-BLEQUES (plural). The basic fabric and cut remain the same, the embroidery patterns and colors may be different: red, black, blue, and purple are seen. There is another female costume called LA MONTUNO or "man killer" worn in the interior areas of Ocú and Las Tablas. It consists of the same hat as the man's, same blouse as the Pollera in a simpler form, and a floral print skirt with a deep lower flounce.

> 11" Maker unknown (doll by Reliable) Canada (costuming) Panama 1966
>
> Plastic swivel head, blue plastic sleep eyes (painted eyebrows, mouth and mustache on man), painted black hair (Male), black mohair wig (Female), plastic body with jointed arms
>
> RELIABLE // MADE IN CANADA // PAT. 1958 (back)

Panamanian couple in best costume, 1959.

PAPUA–NEW GUINEA

13" Metti/Netta Adelaide, Australia 1970s
Vinyl swivel head, green plastic sleep eyes, open/closed mouth with teeth, black synthetic hair, vinyl body with jointed arms and legs
METTI // AUSTRALIA
Courtesy of the Rosalie Whyel Museum of Doll Art

About the Doll

In the 1970s the Australian company Metti/Netta produced a series of 13" vinyl dolls to be dressed and sold by the various native peoples of the highland areas (around Mt. Hagan) of Papua-New Guinea. The dolls have chubby bodies and broadly smiling faces that are cute and naive enough that they don't edge over the line into caricatures. The costuming is truly wonderful; it is realistically-designed and made from woven grass, raffia, rags, beads, and tiny shells. Each face is hand-painted with tribal markings. Marjory Fainges, a fine Australian friend, shows more examples of these dolls in *The Encyclopedia of Regional Dolls*.

Costume Description

He wears woven straw and seeds and bark cloth. The face painting indicates a special occasion.

One of the headdresses of Papua–New Guinea, early 20th century.

PERU

About the Doll

Peruvian dolls like this one, with expressively-modeled papier-mâché heads, are frequently found and seem to have been made over a long period of time. Kimport shows similar Peruvian dolls in their catalogs of the 1930s and 1940s. Dolls of the same style can still be found today, although the quality is considerably diminished.

A 1984 article by Mary Hathaway in *National Doll World* illustrates a similar recent doll made by the Ciprian and Julia Amexquita family of Peru. The head is papier-mâché and the body is papier-mâché over a wire armature. The whole family, as with many cottage industry-type makers, gets into the act: father models the doll, mother paints the face, and mother and daughters make the clothing.

Costume Description

He wears a truncated cone wool hat over a knitted cap; white shirt; woven poncho; black knee pants and, in hand, a staff of office. Wool is the dominant fabric used for these costumes.

Mayor from Cuzco, Peru holding his staff of office, 1950s.

13" Maker unknown Peru 1940s
Ceramic shoulder head with molded and painted features, painted black hair, thread-wrapped wire body and limbs
Not marked

9-1/2" Maker unknown
Philippines 1960s

Cloth swivel head with painted features, black floss hair, cloth over wire armature body

Not marked

About the Dolls

A Filipino pair fresh from the country is part of a large series of silk-covered dolls depicting various costumes and occupations. These dolls were widely produced by a cottage-type industry (that unfortunately did not mark or tag them), and imported over several decades by companies from Kimport to Mark Farmer. The latter featured a whole page of these dolls in an early 1960s catalog, from country folk to the Spanish-influenced women's "mestiza" costume.

Costume Description

Country attire: his hat is of straw; cotton neckerchief; collarless striped long shirt and brown striped cotton pants.

The woman wears the BATINTAWAK (singular) costume; plaid head kerchief; earrings; necklace; bracelet; green dotted dress with wide net sleeves; a shoulder piece draped over one side; a plaid over-skirt is wrapped around the body and green satin shoes. The prints and colors of her garments may vary, the types of garments will remain the same. These costumes combine native and Spanish ideas of dress.

Sulu Province, Moro people (Mohammedan Malays)

11" Maker unknown
Philippines c.1940

Cloth head with painted and needle-sculpted features, black string hair, unjointed cloth body

Not marked

About the Dolls

Described and illustrated in the Kimport international doll catalog of 1937, the Moro dolls are quite different from the usual Filipino ones. This pair is in excellent condition, with vivid costumes and very little aging. Their faces have just a bit of needle-sculpturing to give them shape, and their large painted eyes and outlined red mouths give them lots of personality.

The author has seen a few other dolls in the obvious style of this maker; one was a lovely mestiza woman, quite a bit larger than these. I forgot to go back and purchase her at the end of an exhausting tour of an antique show; I hope she will be back at the next show! The dealer suggested a date of the 1940s, the same time period as our Moro pair.

Costume Description

Festive wear: sash and turban of yellow plaid taffeta; blue brocade jacket and pants, sequins down the front and at ankle imitate coin buttons.

Her hair in a chignon; white lace under blouse; green brocade jacket with sequins as coin buttons; pink and green plaid taffeta shoulder drape.

10-1/2" Distributed by Cepelia Union of Handicraft and Folk Art Cooperatives
Poland 1960s

Composition shoulder head with painted features, blonde floss wigs,
cloth body over wire armature

Not marked

Krakow costume finery, Poland, mid 20th century.

Krakow Department

About the Dolls (see pages 116-117)

The maker of these often-seen Polish dolls, found singly or as dancing pairs on a single base, is not yet identified. The dolls have been produced over at least a thirty year period, and were at one point distributed by the Cepelia Union of Handicrafts. Kimport's "Doll Talk" newsletter identified two of the former makers of Polish dolls (see "Janosik" the Carpathian bandit [on page 118] under Poland), but not this more recent company. We show three examples of their style: the pairs from Lowicz and Krakow, and the single girl (of a slightly earlier date), also from Lowicz. They are attractive dolls, and readily available to the collector, but lack the passion and fire of older dolls like "Janosik."

Costume Description

Woman wears floral crown over braided hair; white full sleeved blouse with lace frill at the neck and wrist. Black bodice with beads and tassels. Red beads imitating real coral; red gathered skirt with floral motifs; white net apron and black boots.

Krakow man's festive wear: man in squared red hat with ribbons and peacock feathers; white

Continued on page 117.

KRAKOWIACY

POLAND

Lowicz Commune, Warszawa Department

9" — 10" Distributed by Cepelia Union of Handicraft and Folk Art Cooperatives Poland 1950s-1966

Composition shoulder head with painted features, blonde human hair wig, cloth body over wire armature

LALKA LOWICKA // KT 37.3 // GATI // CENA DEL (date of 12-20-66 also inscribed)

full sleeved shirt; red and white striped baggy pants tucked into black boots; blue sleeveless coat trimmed with red edging and tassels; white belt with metal disks hanging from the hip.

Costume Description

Lowicz festive wear: man wears black hat with decorative band and pompons; white full sleeved shirt with collar and cuffs; gold buttoned, hip length, black vest trimmed in red-orange, tied with sash. Red-orange striped, medium full trousers tucked into black boots.

Woman in red kerchief tied in back over braids; white full sleeved blouse with collar and cuffs embroidered at upper arm; black wool or velvet bodice usually embroidered and beaded in flowers; red beads at the neck imitate coral. Gathered skirt and apron are woven in multicolored wool, trimmed with lace, sequins, and soutache; black boots. The wide border with embroidered flowers is a more recent development. Red kerchief would hide most of the hair as it does on one of our examples. Kerchief is sometimes white or yellow with flowers worn at the temple. Short laced boots may be worn instead of the taller boots.

ŁOWICZANIE

Couple in woven fabrics from Lowicz in Poland, mid 20th century.

Carpathian Mountains

About the Doll

The dashing and romantic dark-eyed "Anton" hails from the wild Carpathian mountains, found in countries from Poland to Romania to the Ukraine. He is actually a portrait of Janosik, a legendary Robin Hood-type bandit.

His original tag (not shown) shows that he was purchased from Bullock's (a Los Angeles department store) as part of their "Dolls from Many Lands." According to Ethelyn McKim (verbal communication, 1995), Kimport wholesaled their international dolls to several companies including Bullock's.

In an article in "Doll Talk" (Aug.-Sept. 1942) called "The Dolls of Poland," Kimport mourns the loss of a Polish company to Hitler's invasion of Warsaw. They speak longingly of the "utterly lovely" dolls of Zygmunt K. Allina. Allina provided, in a range of ten sizes, men and women from about six different Polish districts.

Allina dolls included Hutzul people of the Tatra Mountains; Silesians; Gorale Mountain people wearing richly embroidered and beaded clothing and tooled leather shoes, wedding pairs from Krakow that were "sheer triumph of doll maker's art," and of course our "fabulously handsome" Janosik, with "tightly swathed and shapely ankles!" (Kimport, *ibid.*)

I have only seen a few of the Allina dolls in the course of researching this book, and must agree with Kimport's glowing compliments. The doll maker lavished their dolls with pride and obvious love.

Costume Description

This historical figure became a folk hero known by several names. He seems to have been active in the late 17th and early 18th centuries as a kind of Robin Hood. He was captured and hung in 1713 despite his reputation for supernatural powers. He continues to live on, in folk dance and song, as a symbol of the eternal struggle for freedom.

His tall red hat with gold trim demonstrates an earlier style. His hair is shown falling free and it could be worn in several braids. He wears a blue open sleeved shirt with red trim; brown jacket with red trim; wide leather belt with brass studs and buckles; knives and pistols would be thrust into his belt; red pants with black and gold trim and Polish shoes called KIERPCE (plural). He usually carries a mountain axe or two. The color may vary but his garment inventory will remain the same.

8" Zygmunt K. Allina Warsaw, Poland c.1940
Composition head with painted features, side-glancing eyes, black mohair wig, cloth over wire armature body, felt hands with separate fingers and thumbs
(GLOBE SURROUNDED BY DOLLS) // BULLOCK'S // DOLLS FROM // MANY LANDS (paper tag) ANTON, A POLISH // BANDIT, FROM // THE CARPATHIAN MOUNTAINS (inscribed in ink on back of tag)

Viana do Castelo District, Minho Province

About the Doll

Maria Helena's comic-faced Portuguese dolls were probably inspired by the Spanish dolls of Klumpe. Her costumes are well-made and have a lot of handwork. Other Maria Helena dolls include a spinner, herdsman, vegetable seller, fisherman from Nazare, chicken vendor from Lisbon (with a chicken in the basket on her head), and bullfighters. These dolls were sold through Kimport and other importers such as Mark Farmer from the late 1950s into the early 1970s. They are usually very well marked.

Another style of Portuguese doll, not illustrated here but frequently found, is the all yarn doll. These yarn dolls, usually made in smaller sizes, have been available for many decades. Often quite appealing — especially the older dolls, which have impressive wool embroidery and lots of interesting detail.

Costume Description

For the woman a wool head kerchief with fringe is worn covering most of the hair; long sleeved white blouse with blue embroidery on the upper arm; the decoratively woven wool bodice, gathered skirt, apron and skirt-pocket are all ornamented with additional embroidery and sequins. Fancy white knitted knee socks and embroidered mules would be worn; she could have another large kerchief tied across the upper body. Earrings and bead necklaces would be worn. A town name or sentimental phrase is frequently embroidered on the apron.

For the man: black or dark blue felt hat with a red pompon; long sleeved white shirt with red embroidery on the collar; red sash; black felt pants and jacket draped over the shoulder.

Portuguese man and woman of Minho, on 1892 Singer Sewing machine trade card.

Paper tags of Maria Helena dolls.

10-1/2—11" Maria Helena Sintra, Portugal 1960s

Movable cloth head with embroidered features, brown wool wig, cloth body over wire armature, weighted (lead) feet, stitched fingers, separate thumbs

HAND MADE // IN PORTUGAL (red/green flag-shaped paper tag)
MINHO // 112 (reverse of tag)
MASCOTTES // DE // MARIA // HELENA (gold paper tag)

PORTUGAL

Azores (Islands in the Atlantic Ocean)

About the Dolls

Sold in the Kimport catalog of 1939, this cloth pair certainly has the look of 1920s-1930s boudoir or bed dolls, both in their facial painting with elongated eyes, lots of eyeshadow and Cupid's-bow mouths, and in their rather lanky bodies. She is quite dramatic in her large hooded "faldetta" or cape. Her beau cuts quite a dashing figure, himself!

Costume Description

Her good dress consists of a white cotton head kerchief, a white cotton blouse with tucked front; gathered print skirt; brown stockings and brown lace-up shoes. Most striking is the black wool full length cape with collar and separate hood, called a FALDETTA (singular). This garment is still worn on Malta in a slightly different form. It is said to have originated in North Africa as a HUIK (singular) and earlier was worn in more parts of Europe for mourning, under different names and guises.

He wears, set at an angle a tasseled knit cap in orange, brown, and green; collarless white shirt; a three piece brown wool suit banded in black, and brown shoes.

11"—14-1/2" Maker unknown Portugal c.1939

Pressed cloth head with hand-painted features, no hair (Male), brown yarn hair (Female), cloth body with swing-jointed arms and stitched fingers

KIMPORT (cloth tag)

Courtesy of the Rosalie Whyel Museum of Doll Art

Portuguese sun shade with applique
cloth "dolls," mid 20th century.

Bistritza-Nasaud District, Transylvania Region

8-1/2" Coop Arta Crisana Oradea, Romania 1978

Vinyl head with painted features, brown synthetic wig, cloth body with cloth over wire upper arms, vinyl lower arms and legs

COOP ARTA CRISANA ORADEA PAPUSA TARAN BISTRITA // SIMBOL CXV // 322 // MADE IN ROMANIA

Note: "Bistritza" and "Bistrita" are both correct spellings.

About the Dolls

Offered for sale in the United States by Kimport Dolls first in 1970, these nicely-made and detailed small (8-1/2") dolls were still being made (in 1995) for sale in towns in Romania. They are made by the folk arts cooperative "Arta Crisana" in Oradea, Romania; new ones are in boxes marked "Cooperativa Mestesugareasea//'Arta Crisana' Oradea."

The dolls are made of a molded rigid plastic attached to a cloth body, with cloth over wire upper limbs. Hair is made from fine embroidery floss, painting is simple but deft, and clothing is not only quite detailed but to scale. The dolls are found on both clear plastic stands and on wooden bases. Older dolls had a wrist tag noting the maker and their region on a map of Romania. Some dolls, like the male shown here, have the same information on a paper label attached under the base.

It is a tribute to the Romanian people's innate creativity that they were able to create such lovely little dolls, even while under the oppressive rule of harsh Communist dictators.

Costume Description

Festive attire: black felt hat with large ornament of peacock feathers to one side; white open sleeved shirt; white pants; leather vest with painted decoration imitating embroidery and multicolored tassels; wide decorative leather belt; black painted boots.

Female festive attire: her hair in one braid; headdress with decorative roundels over the ears; red beads; homespun chemise with full sleeves; leather vest embellished with appliqué and paint; hand-woven double apron, one in front and one in back. The chemise could have more embroidery on the sleeves and chest.

ROMANIA
Mehedintzi District, Oltenia Region

About the Dolls

A really great pair of composition-head Romanian dolls, obviously dressed by hand and with great care. Four of these dolls were purchased at the estate auction of a couple who lived in Bucharest, the capital of Romania, in the 1930s. The dolls' heads were possibly made in Germany; they are of fairly good quality composition with sweetly-painted faces.

This carefree couple is part of a genre referred to as "peasant dolls" in doll books and lady's magazines of the 1930s-40s. The peasants of Old World Europe and their costumes, both vanishing breeds, were considered exotic, romantic and charming. Gypsy clothing and songs were fashionable amongst city-dwelling Americans. Romania is one of the homes of the Romany people, better known as gypsies.

Costume Description

Female festive wear: a white oblong veil called MARAMA (singular); flower in hair; homespun white chemise with sequins and embroidered in red on front, sleeves, and hem; black wool pleated open wrap skirt called VILNIC (singular); ribbon belt; leather Romanian footwear. The skirt is decorated with sequins, to imitate a flat metal ribbon folded into geometric designs. On her shoulder is a wooden yoke to carry two hand-woven bags.

Male festive attire: black karakul hat; white full sleeved cotton shirt with red embroidery on front and cuffs; shirt worn outside the white homespun pants; white leather vest trimmed with black karakul, black felt and red stitching; wide leather belt with metal studs and decorative sewing; red sash worn under belt; blue and white checked leg wrappings; Romanian sandal; hand-woven carry bag and stick.

ROMANIA
Mehedintzi District, Oltenia Region

Back view of Transylvanian sheepskin vest, Romania, circa 1910.

Transylvanian household embroidery, Romania, early 20th century

Opposite page:

12" Maker unknown Romania c.1930s

Composition head with painted blue eyes, brown mohair wig, cloth body with jointed arms and legs

Not marked

The Romanian woman on the right wears the same distinctive costume as our doll, c.1920s

Vyshnyaya Zalegoslich village, Tula Province, Novosilyevsky Region

About the Doll

Alexandra Kukinova of Moscow, 32 years old, was originally a theater costume designer whose interests spilled over into designing cloth dolls in traditional Russian costume. Several years ago Alexandra created a line of dolls with porcelain heads and limbs. Recently she added a line of three very large (35") dolls like our "Anfisa," with ceramic head and limbs and very elaborate folk costumes. Alexandra (her pet name is "Sasha") is pictured here with several of her dolls.

Alexandra's dolls are modeled by leading Russian sculptors; "Anfisa," for instance, was sculpted by "Kazanskaya K." Alexandra also credits her technical advisors for "Anfisa": Oscolcova, Pavlushina, and Umnova. She researches and designs her dolls' costumes with great care and attention to detail.

Costume Description

Newly married woman's 19th century festive costume: many-colored ribbon crown with pompons at the ears; bead and button necklaces; white open sleeve chemise, red

Alexandra Kukinova with some of her Russian doll creations, including our "Anfisa," 1995.

sleeves ornamented with braid trim in red, white, and ochre yellow; large window pane checked blue skirt, red border and ribbon rosettes in bright colors on back; dark blue-green, bodice-like, upper garment with pleated back, trimmed in metallic braid and ribbon; multicolor fabric sash hangs down in front; bast shoes. Original costume is in the State Museum of Ethnography in St. Petersburg.

Opposite Page:

35" Alexandra Kukinova Moscow, Russia 1995

Ceramic shoulder head with molded breasts, blue glass eyes with lashes, closed mouth, cloth body, cloth legs and upper arms, ceramic lower arms

ALEXANDRA // RUSSIA // MOSCOW (cloth tag on underclothes)

15" Maker unknown Russia 1920s-1930s
Pressed stockinet head with painted blue eyes, no hair, cloth body with swing-jointed arms and legs
MADE IN RUSSIA // MORDWA WOMAN (cloth tag sewn to underclothes)

Mordvia Autonomous Republic

About the Doll

A serene stockinet-faced woman from the Mordvia Autonomous Republic is one of a series of these dolls from Russia. They are fascinating and handsome, yet information about them is very elusive. We do not yet know the maker and possibly never will; the Soviet Union encouraged traditional crafts but not the individual worker. Arts and crafts were organized into cooperatives with high-flown socialistic names. Now, with the dissolution of the Soviet Union, any such information is apt to be lost. But we keep looking for that scrap of information, that key....

A book about the doll collection at the Wenham Museum written in 1951 by Adeline Cole shows a small black and white photograph of a "complete" (?) set of 13 adults in the large (14"-15") size of the stockinet dolls.

The set includes: Belarus, Esquimaux (Eskimo from Siberia) man and woman, Kursk, Mordva, Orlovskiy, Ryazan, a Samoyed, a shepherd, Smolensk, Ukraine, Voronezh and others. A "village boy" (misspelled "willage" on the tags) is shown in our foreword, but is not found in the Wenham photograph. These dolls were made from about 1920 to the 1940s; earlier dolls are marked "Made in Russia" or "Foreign Made"; ones after 1922 (when the USSR was created) are marked "Soviet Union."

Kimport sold these, plus other sizes of the stockinet dolls: 6-1/2", 8-1/2", and 10" children in various costumes plus 4" sizes with composition heads and limbs. The quality of the composition on these tiny dolls is poor; it is really a pity because they have beautiful little character-like faces. Kimport had such a problem with the easily-damaged dolls that they finally sold out the damaged ones for a pittance (75 cents per pair).

Other Russian stockinet dolls from this period include "tea cozies" (with quilted skirts to keep a pot of tea warm) in several sizes and an unusually-large 26" doll with long soft limbs and full skirts like a 1920s boudoir or "bed" doll.

Costume Description

A Finnic people, female dress: linen turban headdress ends in bright colors with bead and rabbit fur pompons; green, black and silver necklace; beige linen long sleeved chemise worn in blouson style, stenciled designs at all openings and the under arm gussets; green cord belt attached with bright stenciled pink and green kerchiefs; cotton leg wrappings and bast shoes.

*Please Note: Mordvia, Mordva and Mordwa are correct spellings.

Ryazan Region

About the Doll

Dolls from several different German makers, including Kämmer and Reinhardt, were used in Zagorsk, Russia to make a series of Russian-costumed dolls from the late 1800s through the 1920s. The dolls were imported to Russia and costumed (and possibly assembled) in Zagorsk. The doll on the next page is one of the earlier examples with a bisque head, quality German composition ball-jointed body, porcelain teeth and German glass eyes. She is marked "448," which is not a documented Kämmer and Reinhardt number, but her head is very similar to other "dolly-faced" heads produced by porcelain maker Simon & Halbig for Kämmer & Reinhardt.

Zagorsk, northeast of Moscow, a picturesque old Russian town formerly known as Sergiev Posad, has long been the Russian center for doll and toy making. In the late 19th century, according to *Russian Folk Toys* — a catalogue by the museum of toys in Zagorsk, interest in Russian antiques and folk culture inspired a series of dolls dressed in costumes from various Russian provinces.

Later dolls (1920s and '30s), one of which is pictured here under Ukraine, were very likely also made in Zagorsk under the new Soviet regime. These charming but inferior quality dolls, made in ceramic rather than bisque, were presumably completely produced in Russia (the USSR), utilizing leftover Kämmer and Reinhardt molds. See remarks under Ukraine for more information on these ceramic-head dolls.

Costume Description

Festive costume: hair in single braid; wool challis kerchief tied on head, red crown trimmed in gold braid; metal earrings and glass necklace; white linen full sleeved chemise with red embroidery on sleeve and printed fabric trim at hem, chest, shoulder and underarm gussets; red wool skirt, yellow ribbon and green cord edge; white linen apron top, red woven lower part ending in lace; multicolored striped sash; wrapped legs and leather shoes.

*Photograph of doll appears on page 128.

Russian woman in traditional dress of Ryazan Province, early 20th century.

> 19" Kämmer & Reinhardt Waltershausen, Germany
> Costumed & possibly assembled in Zagorsk
> (previously Sergiev Posad), Russia c.1900
>
> Bisque socket head, blue sleep eyes, open mouth with teeth, blonde mohair wig, ball-jointed composition body 448 (back of head)
>
> *Pat Foster collection*

Late 19th century Russian ceremonial towel, linen with cross-stitch embroidery in red and black, crochet border.

Kämmer & Reinhardt doll in costume of Ryazan, Russia. *Pat Foster collection. See page 127.*

RUSSIA

Yakutia Autonomous Republic, Siberia

11" Maker unknown Siberia, Russia 1964-65

Carved wooden head with painted features, dark brown fur hair, unjointed cloth body

(Transliterated) YAKUTZ // 73 // OOMP(?) // ROCKPS(?) // PETROPAVLOVSK-KAMCHATSKIY // SOUVENIR // SHAMAN // ART. (on base)

Jaye Delbridge collection

About the Doll

An exotic Yakutz doll from Siberia, crafted — obviously with great care, for the 1964-65 New York World's Fair where he was purchased. A talented wood carver created this compelling portrait of a powerful figure, perhaps a real man. Dolls actually made in Siberia are rare and, like many ethnic dolls, vary greatly in quality. We were thrilled to find this wonderful example.

Costume Description

Male dancer with drum: hat, bib, parka, and boots are all of fur and leather. Ornamentation is in appliqué and beadwork.

SAUDI ARABIA

(Female) The Najd (Heart of the Kingdom)

About the Dolls

Mrs. Alma Fritzi reported that she and her husband lived in Dhahran, Saudi Arabia about 1939-1947, where her husband worked. Although Saudis do not generally make dolls or figures resembling humans because their Muslim religion prohibits it, Alma was still able to get these dolls made for her through the help of her houseboy. She tells a story of "smuggling" the dolls out when she left!

The dolls are rather simple cloth affairs with embroidered faces and yarn hair. Above her veil, the female's eyes are large and dark with mystery.

Costume Description

Festive finery — BANI TAMIM Dress: woman in a very wide sleeved gown called a THAWB (singular) of red chiffon with gold braid and trim; a mauve rayon under gown; a long black net scarf called SHAYLA (singular); pantaloons in a blue print called SIR-

WAAL (singular). Again, the terms are varied and will be different from place to place.

His head is swathed in a red and white head wrap called a GHOUTRA (singular) and held by a black band, the IGAAL (singular). The wrap could be in black and white. There is a white rayon under robe with gold trim called THAWB (singular), a rust colored over robe called GUMBAZ (singular); white cotton under pantaloons called SIRWAAL (singular).

There are localized names for all the garments and alternate names for them as well. The form of the clothes remains the same, but the richness can increase with the wealth of the owner.

> 13-1/4"   Maker unknown   Dhahran, Saudi Arabia   c.1945
> Cloth head with embroidered features, black yarn hair, cloth body, not jointed
> No marks
> *Courtesy of the Rosalie Whyel Museum of Doll Art*

SENEGAL

Wolof people

About the Doll

A fascinating and fabulous lady doll created ever-so-briefly by the French master doll maker, Leon Casimir Bru. Her bisque head with its distinctly modeled ethnic features was produced for Bru by French porcelain maker Eugene-Constant Barrois. The doll's kid leather body is tinted very dark brown to match her complexion.

She is swathed in layer after contrasting layer of bright, hand-woven textiles and fancy silks like her human counterpart (shown in the engraving), making her slender body appear massive, especially in comparison to her head! Custom-made leather thong-type sandals grace her feet. Underneath her third inner skirt, strands of red and white cased-glass trade beads are wound around her body, allowing her to carry some of her wealth with her. A demure silver mesh purse, incongruous enough to mean it is probably original, completes the exotic ensemble.

Dolls like this Wolof woman from Senegal by Bru are a very rare breed—only a few are known. She was probably part of a French exhibit for a world fair, created to show the French possessions in Africa.

Costume Description

The Wolof controlled a great empire in the 15th century and were early converts to Islam. She shows a green turban with decorative balls in front; gold earrings and necklace; under robe with white eyelet borders; over robe of sheer multicolored brocade; horizontal striped wrap skirt with fringe. There are more under robes and striped under skirts; these are style and wealth indicators.

*Photograph of doll appears on page 132.

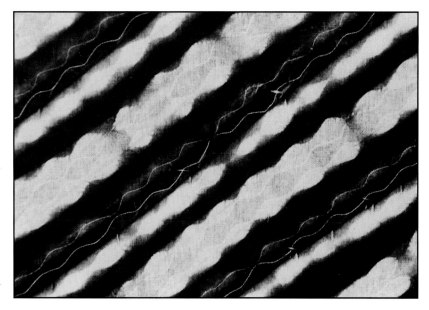

West African cotton resist-dyed fabric, 20th century.

19th century etching of Wolof women from what is today Senegal.

SENEGAL

Wolof people

Doll by Bru in costume of Senegal. *Rosalie Whyel Museum of Doll Art. See page 131.*

Cicmany, Trecianska Area, western Slovakia

About the Doll

Our Slovakian girl was purchased at the "Jizba Krasna" store in a tiny courtyard off Wenceslaus Square in Prague. They specialized in handmade folk arts. Although we could speak to the salesperson in some German, she was not able to tell us who made this doll, which was one of about six in different Czech and Slovak costumes. The doll's head is made of a rigid plastic which looks like celluloid, with simply-painted (and greatly varying from doll to doll) features.

A rather extensive search for other handmade dolls in Prague was disappointing. There were many types of marionettes, plus lots of the nice but commercially made-vinyl dolls of the Lidova Tvorba company, but not many other dolls of the handmade variety.

Couple from Trecianska in the Slovak Republic (Slovakia), early 20th century.

Costume Description

Young girl: hair worn in a single braid; white cotton full sleeved blouse with pleated body, lace ruffle at neck and wrist, red and yellow embroidery on upper arm. The pleated skirt called RUBAC (singular), could have an embroidered waist band; gathered embroidered apron has lace edging and inserts. Red stockings and native shoes. The embroidery could have more ochre yellow. If married, she would wear an embroidered cap. The women paint the outside walls of the house with the embroidery motifs.

9" Distributed by Jizba Krasna Prague, Czech Republic 1990s
Plastic swivel head with painted blue eyes, black floss hair in long braid, stockinet body over wire armature, separate thumb and stitched fingers
Not marked

SPAIN

Andalucia Region

About the Dolls

A hand-written note on the back of the doll maker's card is translated: "A gift from the Mariquita Perez firm for the granddaughter of President Eisenhower." This pair of dolls was a gift to the President on his state visit with Spanish President Franco in 1959. According to *Pollock's Dictionary of English Dolls*, Mariquita Perez Sociedad Anónima registered the trademark "Mariquita Perez" in England in 1948 for dolls and dolls' clothes (p. 206).

The dolls are quite marvelous and well-dressed, especially the boy! He has a wardrobe of clothing (not illustrated) from various regions of Spain, plus an elaborate costume of a torero (bullfighter). The clothing is very well-made, rivaling the best fashions of any self-respecting late 1950s doll, with tiny snap closures and buttonholes, embroidery and gold sequin encrustation, ruffled shirts with rhinestone buttons, hand-cobbled shoes, a bagpipe for his Galicia costume, and classy hats.

Flirting eyes, open mouths with teeth, swivel waists, and human hair are all a part of these deluxe quality dolls, made for their special Presidential presentation.

Costume Description

Man in black felt low crowned hat; white cotton ruffled shirt with band collar and gold buttons; grey jacket with black velvet collar and braid trim; red sash and black wool pants.

The girl wears a red and white dotted Flamenco dress with white ruffles; red fringed shawl; jewelry which includes gold combs and beads; carries white plastic castanets; colors and prints of dress and shawl may be of great variety.

These outfits would be seen everywhere in Seville during Holy Week celebrations.

18" Mariquita Perez Sociedad Anónima Madrid, Spain 1959
Mâché over plastic socket head, blue plastic flirty eyes, open mouth with teeth, bown human hair, mâché over plastic body, jointed arms and legs, swivel waist
MARIQUITA PEREZ // IMPUESTO DELUJO METALICO // PERMISO NO 908 (paper wrist tag) MARIQUITA PEREZ (stamped on body)
Courtesy of the Rosalie Whyel Museum of Doll Art

SPAIN
Valencia Province

About the Doll

The lady of Valencia — romantic, exotic and even more sumptuously-painted and shaded than many Lenci dolls. Unfortunately, we know so much about the dolls by Lenci and so woefully little about this doll's maker — Pages of Madrid. The doll is definitely from the 1920s or early 1930s with her long-limbed, languid elegance. She was obviously an expensive doll with her sequin-trimmed silk and lace dress, brass hair combs, and leather high heels. Perhaps a reader will know these dolls; or perhaps a future trip to Spain and dig in Madrid's archives will help explain our enigmatic Spanish señora.

Costume Description

Lady in special hair arrangement of braided roundels around each ear and in back with many decorative combs, a pin, bracelets, and other matching jewelry. Pastel brocade floral dress with low cut neck and lace at the elbow; lace embroidered and sequined fichu and apron; two pastel colored bows falling from the upper shoulder-back and the waist; pastel brocade shoes with bright pompons. Earlier this area boasted a greater variety of costumes.

*Another photograph of the doll appears on page 136.

133 - Labradoras valencianas a la antigua usanza

Spanish ladies of Valencia in best dress, c.1930s.

Above and next page:

20" Pages, S.A. (Inc.) Madrid, Spain 1920s

Pressed felt head, painted side-glancing brown eyes, eyeshadow above/under eyes, red lips, brown mohair wig in side coils, cloth body with jointed arms and legs, fingers separate except 2nd and 3rd

JUGUETES Y MUÑECAS // PAGES, S.A. // GENERAL PARITER 29-MADRID (SPAIN) (paper tag on underclothes)

Valencia woman by Pages, S.A. of Spain. *See page 135.*

SPAIN

Alburquerque, Badajoz Province, Extremadura Region

About the Doll

Exquisitely hand-painted, with handwork flourishes such as the coiled bun at the back of her head and paper flower tucked behind one ear, she is another of the very special and unique dolls from Spain. For a country not particularly noted for their dolls, Spain has produced some beautiful ones (of which we still know almost nothing).

This lady's tag indicates she was purchased at the Market for Spanish Artisans; other details coded on her tag probably once revealed her maker and where she was made. "Jaen," written on the tag, is a town in Spain but not within the area which the doll's costume represents.

It is a great pity to lose the names of talented artists such as the one who made this doll.

Costume Description

Female daily dress in an older style. Hair worn in high braided chignon, roses at her temple; red wool triangle worn over the head; black and white woven horizontal striped skirt with braided hem; fine cotton embroidered shawl; black velvet bodice-with-sleeves; blue and white cotton apron and embroidered stockings.

12-1/2" Maker unknown Spain c.1930s
Composition swivel head with hand-painted features, brown mohair wig, composition body jointed at arms and legs
A // R-M/TE // P-JAEN // MERCADOS DE LA ARTESANA ESPAÑOL (paper wrist tag)

Spanish dancers of Badajoz, 1950s.

SPAIN

Lagartera, Toledo Province

SPAIN

About the Dolls

The dolls by "Klumpe" of Barcelona, Spain are a delight to look at, both for their quality and their comic relief. From the coy courtship of this pair of Spanish lovers, to the comic bravado of a bullfighter, to passionate dancers of the flamenco, Klumpe made wonderful little funny felt dolls representing peoples of the regions of Spain.

With Klumpe and its imitators — Roldan, Niste and others, no one else was spared from their witty touches. The well-heeled shopper with an equally-snooty poodle, golfers, an exasperated mother-to-be, and even doctors and nurses — simply everyone got a dose of Klumpe's arch-eyebrowed, rolling-eyed humor.

Couple from Toledo in Spain, 1950s.

Costume Description

Woman in white head kerchief; beads on neck and ears; black bodice-with-sleeves; black apron; red felt ornamental shawl; red skirt decorated with braids, trims, sequins; bright striped stockings.

Man wearing black felt hat with red band and green and red pompons; white shirt; black sequin buttons; black velvet jacket and knee pants with a wide purple sash.

SURINAM

About the Doll

The country of Surinam was formerly Dutch Guiana and one can certainly see the European influence in her "Mother Hubbard" costume. However, the primitive but cute doll, with her uniquely-shaped "nosy" face and quite shapely body beneath the padding of layers of her clothing, is definitely the artist's very own style!

Costume Description

The KOTO MISSIE dress derives from that introduced by missionaries. All outer garments are of a red printed cotton; the odd-shaped turban, over blouse and skirt. Necklace and earrings would be gold; white lace under blouse and pale blue cotton petticoat. Both the petticoat and skirt are folded down at the top to form a wide peplum, adding to the girth of our lady. The garments and cut will be the same, but the colors and prints will differ, although some kind of stripe seems to be a preferred element. A colorful neckerchief could be worn as well.

Woman from Surinam, c.1940s.

SWAZILAND

About the Doll

An imaginative doll, the Swazi woman perches quite precariously on her broom straw bottom, her big hair threatening to pull her over backwards! Alas, but this tenuous hold on gravity is what also creates her very upright, regal air! She is a quite simple and easily-made tourist doll and yet, like many of the hand-crafted dolls in this book, she is imbued with the grand spirit of the people she represents.

Costume Description

Tall black headwear, pink ribbon; black, white, and red print wrap dress fastens at the shoulder; belt of brown and black wool — this unseen in photo.

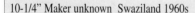

10-1/4" Maker unknown Swaziland 1960s

Cloth head with black yarn features, black cloth wig, cloth upper torso and unjointed arms, broom straw lower torso (no legs)

MADE IN // SWAZILAND (hand-written on paper tag)

Swazi women and children,
mid 20th century.

SWEDEN

Rättvik, Dalecarlia Region, Kopparberg Province

About the Doll

Wearing the most often-seen Swedish costume, from Rättvik, this celluloid pair were imported into the U.S. by Kimport Dolls and sold in the late 1930s. They came with or without fur-trimmed white leather coats, the former being Kimport's "deluxe" models. The Rättvik costume is seen repeatedly on dolls, from antique ones to the present. Its distinctive cap with pompons and the horizontally-striped apron-like panel of the girl are important clues to identifying the many dolls in this costume.

An actual child's costume (missing its cap) is shown here for comparison.

The dolls' celluloid shoulder heads are high quality work by a German company with the cumbersome name "Rheinische Gummi- und Celluloid-Fabrik". This was later changed to "Schildkröte" due to their distinctive "turtle mark" logo ("Schildkröte" = turtle).

Since the dolls are marked "Made in Sweden," a Swedish company must have assembled the German celluloid parts onto cloth bodies, and added their distinctive garments.

Costume Description

Woman's black felt conical hat, red wool trim and pompons; floral printed neckerchief banded in green fastened with metal pin; white long sleeved blouse; green printed minimal bodice with decorative bodice hooks and banded in red; fur trimmed white leather jacket; navy blue gathered skirt with multicolored woven panel; felt skirt-pocket; red stockings; black shoes.

Earlier this hat was worn by the unmarried women and a white cap by the married women. This is the one used today. This skirt panel had a woven apron over it in the 19th century.

Black felt hat with red band ending in pompons; white cotton shirt; brown leather apron; white leather coat with fur edging; yellow sateen pants with red wool garters and pompons; black stockings and buckle shoes. The doll maker has not made the vest or jacket.

Girl's Rättvik costume from Sweden, c. 1906.

11" Maker unknown (head by Schildkröte) Sweden (celluloid parts made in Germany) c.1940

Celluloid shoulder head, blue glass sleep eyes, open mouth with teeth, blonde mohair wig, cloth body with swing-jointed arms and legs, celluloid lower arms

(TURTLE IN DIAMOND) // 8" (head) MADE IN SWEDEN (paper label, sewn-on) KIMPORT (cloth label sewn to clothes)

Family from Rättvik in Sweden, c.1905.

SWEDEN

Ingelstad Harad (village), Skåne Region, Kristianstadt and Malmohus Provinces

Center Front: 6-1/2" Charlotte Weibull Malmo (later Akarp), Sweden 1975

Stockinet-covered ball-shaped swivel head with painted features, blonde yarn wig, cloth body over wire armature

CHARLOTTE // WEIBULL

Courtesy of the Rosalie Whyel Museum of Doll Art

Left and Right: 12" Charlotte Weibull Akarp, Sweden 1995

Stockinet over foam ball head with hand-painted blue eyes, blonde cotton floss wig, foam-wrapped body over wire armature, stockinet hands. Female has no legs (stands on dowel and base)

CHARLOTTE WEIBULL AKARP SWEDEN (circular paper sticker on base of female doll, surrounds drawing of dolls from Skåne region)

SWEDEN

Ingelstad Harad (village), Skåne Region, Kristianstadt and Malmohus Provinces

About the Dolls

Charlotte Weibull, creator of Swedish folk and storybook dolls, began her career in a shop which made the folk costumes of her native region of Skåne. She sold commercially-made dolls in Swedish dress but later, at the suggestion of a tourist, decided to try making her own. In 1958 her first original dolls were offered, and were so much a success that dolls became her most important creations.

According to an article written in 1983 (Campbell, "Sweden's Charlotte Weibull," *Doll Reader®,* Oct. 1983), the workshop at Akarp then employed 25 women to assemble the dolls. The heads are a flesh-colored stockinet over a ball made of a plastic compound. Special fabrics were woven, and about 100 seamstresses around the country sewed costumes and dressed the dolls, sending them to Charlotte's workshop for finishing.

The larger pair shown here were specially made in 1995 for this book (the larger sizes are not common); the smaller doll was purchased in 1975. The tall pair wear the costumes of Ingelstadt Harad in Skåne, the farming region of Charlotte's birth and still her home and workshop. A Skåne boy and girl are illustrated in Charlotte Weibull's logo (see photo).

Costume Description

Festive dress: tall black felt hat, velvet hat band and flower; ribbon tie; white long sleeved shirt with lace at the neck and cuffs; yellow suede cloth vest and knee pants with black buttons; black velvet jacket with green and red embroidery, and wooden shoes.

Particular red cloth female headdress; pin at the neck; white long sleeved blouse; gathered red wool skirt with black velvet band near hem; black velvet bodice decorated with gold braid and beads; black felt jacket with green trim and large silver buttons; multicolored woven apron; striped woven sash.

Charlotte Weibull with some of her Swedish dolls.
Courtesy Charlotte Weibull.

Charlotte Weibull's logo, with a Skåne boy and girl, is part of the doll's label.

SWITZERLAND

Emmental, Berne Canton

About the Doll

A very interesting and unusual cloth body construction for this papier-mâché doll with her early and ornate Swiss costume from Berne. Her cloth body is "hinged" at the juncture of the derriere and legs, allowing her to easily sit; cloth tabs then can hold her in a sitting position. Her sweet, pointy-chinned head is of a high quality, with inset glass eyes.

Note the comparison of her costume, with green striped silk apron, beaded black bodice, puffy sleeved blouse and net lower sleeves, with the postcard illustrating the early 19th century costume of Berne. A newer Swiss wooden doll and later postcard, on the next page, show the Berne costume which evolved in the 20th century.

Costume Description

19th century holiday dress. Emmental and Mittelland have very similar attire. Black velvet cap with black lace halo called SCHLAPPE (singular); black lace mitts; silver bodice chains, rosettes, and hooks all in filigree. White full sleeved blouse; black velvet or wool bodice worn usually with a similar partlet (a separate yoke); long gathered black skirt; striped green and cream gathered apron was in fashion in the 18th and 19th centuries. An organization to preserve and recreate Swiss costumes is called the Federation Nationale des Costumes Suisses, formed in 1926.

14" Maker unknown Germany c.1850
Papier-mâché shoulder head with inset brown glass eyes, brown human hair wig, cloth body and limbs, back of body is hinged for sitting
Not marked
Courtesy of the Rosalie Whyel Museum of Doll Art

BERN

19th century festive dress from Berne canton.

Emmental, Berne Canton

About the Doll

Laura Knusli's research has uncovered the company of Adolf and Paul Thomann of Brienz, Switzerland. Finally, we know who made the type of carved wooden doll shown here. The Thomanns produced these dolls and sold them to other shops to dress in regional Swiss costumes and sell until 1960, when the dolls were sold in Thomann's shop only. Our doll bears the wrist tag of "Johanna" of Lugano, the store that dressed and sold her.

Her body construction, consisting of ten wooden pieces jointed at neck, shoulders, elbows, hips and knees, is very typical of one of three main types of dolls made by the Thomanns. The other types were: (1) a jointed all wood body similar to the above but with slanted hip joints and (2) a German cloth body with wooden head and lower arms (no longer available after

---

10-1/2" Adolf & Paul Thomann Studio Brienz, Switzerland c.1950s

Wooden swivel head with carved features, painted brown eyes, carved and painted brown hair with bun at back, 10 piece all wood body, peg-jointed at elbows and knees, jointed with screws at shoulders and hips

JOANNA // LUGANO (paper wrist tag) MADE IN // BERN // SWITZERLAND (reverse of paper tag)

the beginning of World War II). For more information, see Knüsli, "Swiss Wooden Dolls from Brienz," in *Doll Reader*®, February 1995.

Costume Description

Sunday dress in the 20th century: black cap with lace halo tied under the chin; white full sleeved sheer blouse; black bodice with chain lacing and partlet (separate yoke) on shoulders; black gathered skirt; red gathered apron; all simplified over time. This is the costume most used to represent Switzerland, although there are hundreds more of greater complexity and interest.

Young girl in an early 20th century costume from Berne Canton, Switzerland.

Appenzell Canton

About the Doll

Atelier Baitz was founded in Berlin in 1912. Following World War II, the company moved first to Bad Aussee (Austria) and then to Bregenz, Austria. There it was purchased in 1963 by the current owner Camillo Gärdtner & Company, retaining the "Baitz" name for the doll line. Ten years later they moved to Felling in southern Austria, where they currently still produce about 300 models of international and historical dolls, with two hand-painted faces — a closed mouth, smiling one and the well-known "kissing" one. I am grateful to Camillo Gärdtner's wife, Erika, for all of this information.

The 9" tall Baitz dolls have heads made of a plastic-type material which looks like and is finished like wood. This unbreakable material is unique to Baitz and the exact constituents are kept secret. Their bodies are cloth over wire armature.

I have thus far found Baitz dolls that are dated as far back as the 1950s; this example was purchased in Lucerne, Switzerland in 1967.

Costume Description

Sunday dress: Headdress is of black tulle with white lace insert over a cap of gold lace; short puff sleeve blouse with frill at elbow; gathered red skirt; pink brocade apron usually of silk; white stockings and black shoes. Her shoes may have buckles and stockings may be mauve or red. A long sleeved jacket may be worn.

9" Baitz Els, Austria 1967
Plastic-like swivel head, painted side-glancing eyes, mouth open in an "O" shape, brown mohair wig in coiled bun at back, cloth body with felt arms over wire armature
Not marked

Swiss children from Appenzell, 1921.

SYRIA

(Left to right) Druse woman & baby

About the Dolls (see pages 149-150)

Baronne Sandra Belling was a Russian noblewoman, said to have been born in 1864, who made dolls—"portrait puppets" of court ladies in elegant gowns under the old Russian czarist regime (Kimport, "Doll Talk", undated c. 1940). Exiled to Syria after the Russian Revolution, Belling (in the 1930s) began to teach ballet and doll-making to the wealthier families of Damascus. For her own dolls, she worked with a group of native Syrian women to create Syrian and other Middle Eastern dolls. Belling modeled the faces, which were then covered with stockinet and painted, while the local women made the clothing. Her work somewhat resembles her contemporary, Bernard Ravca of France; it is entirely possible that she saw his work, as Syria was under French mandate rule until 1946. Or instead, she may have developed the style entirely on her own.

Baronne Belling's dolls of the 1930s-50s represented Druse people of the mountains, Bedouins, Damascus dwellers, various Bethlehem sects, even the Syrian gypsy fortune teller with her child seen here on the right. The Krug International Doll House also sold the Belling dolls, and in a 1947 newsletter mentions a family of three, a Druse musician, and princess. These sold in the rather steep price range of $12.50 to $15 (antique bisque dolls could be had for much the same).

The dolls are often stamped with Baronne Belling's mark, but confusion arises because the apparent exporter, Arouani Brothers of Damascus, sewed their own identifying tag right over her name. This was apparently an okay thing to do in Syria; after all, Sandra Belling was only a woman! Kimport seemed to sense this disparity, and broke a long-standing policy of not revealing the artist or manufacturer's name (for obvious business reasons) to talk about Ms. Belling.

"Allah be praised—they're perfect!" raves the 1940 Kimport catalog about Baronne Sandra Belling's dolls. And I will break my own rule of impartiality for this book to tell you that these are some of my personal favorites. Detail of costume, fine fabrics, great character of face—these dolls have it all!

Costume Description

Tied around her head is a striped silk turban, coins top the back of the turban; baby in bright print carrier. Our woman wears her hair in braids; metal and bead earrings; yellow cotton undergarment; flounced dress in Bursa silk with long sleeves and slit in front to the waist; black sateen coat, embroidered at sleeve and lower border; red print petticoat and yellow brocade pantaloons.

*Photograph of dolls appear on page 150.

Close up of a doll by Baronne Sandra Belling shown on page 150.

Syrian bedouin woman, c.1905.

SYRIA

(Left to right) Durgin man & woman, Druse woman & baby

Costume Description (for two dolls on left)

The groom's head wear is a red TARBOOSH (fez or hat) with white wrapping around and flowing down; blue and white striped robe; multicolored silk sash; brown cotton short sleeve over-robe; white muslin pantaloons and black shoes.

Bride has a black head wrap which falls over shoulders; a gathered wrap skirt; a pink striped silk dress; bright yellow brocade petticoat and bright yellow pantaloons.

*Costume description for right-hand doll is on page 149.

Above and page 149:

10"—12" Baronne Sandra Belling Damascus, Syria c.1940

Molded head covered with stockinet, hand-painted features, baby's head is celluloid, black yarn hair, cloth over wire armature body, separated fingers

MADE IN SYRIA // AROUANI BROTHERS // DAMASCUS, SYRIA (cloth tag)

Akha group (Tibeto-Burman)

About the Dolls

A phone call from friend Harriet Beerfas concerning books on 18th century children's clothing led to my introduction to the dolls of the Thailand hill tribes. One of the partners in the U.S./Thai corporation (which normally works with engineering projects) who stumbled onto these fine dolls, lives in my home state of Washington. So, between Dwight and Harriet, I have been able to watch these dolls develop and flourish.

The cloth doll versions, which represent females and some children of many of the tribes—the Hmong, Mien, Akha, Karen, Lahu, and Lisu, have actually been around for a bit. The dolls were imported by a group called House of Handicrafts in 1992; an article in the October 1992 *Doll Reader®* features some of these dolls. Its author, Loraine Wellman, lists them as being designed by Vanida S. Mongkhone and handmade by Youthana.

The larger and very handsome ceramic dolls photographed here have been developed over the last year (1995); they are finely-crafted and costumed and sell for a reasonable price. For the first time, male dolls are being made. Let us hope that these excellent dolls meet with enough success to guarantee their continued production.

Costume Description

The Akha live in the Yunnan Province of China, Burma, Laos, and have been in North Thailand less than 25 years.

She displays a complex headdress of wool pompons, metal disks, and chains; jewelry of earrings, torque, bracelets, beads, and large disks down the front; black cotton geometric cut jacket, pants, skirt, and belt, all with appliqué in primary colors.

He wears: a black headwrap with pink feather; silver pin with beads, bracelets, and torque (open necklace); black cotton jacket and pants trimmed in red, white, and turquoise appliqué.

*Photograph of doll appears on page 152.

Page 152:

17" Hill Tribes Federation Thailand 1994

Painted ceramic head, painted features, black yarn hair, cloth torso with painted ceramic lower limbs, cloth over wire upper limbs

RMT LTD (THAILAND) // AUTHENTIC HILL TRIBE DOLL // REG. NO: CH-006 // HILL TRIBES FEDERATION // HANDMADE IN THAILAND (paper label on base)

Modern Akha family of Thailand.

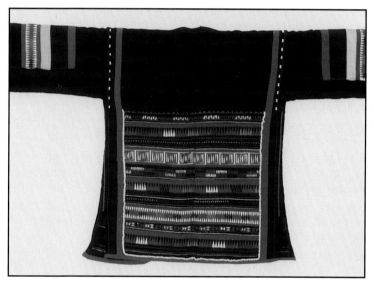

Akha appliqued adult jacket and child's cap, Thailand, mid 20th century.

Akha group (Tibeto-Burman)

Akha dolls by the Hill Tribes Federation. *See page 151.*

TRINIDAD

8"—11" Maker unknown
Trinidad 1960s-1970s

Pressed cloth head with painted features, black mohair wig, cloth over wire armature body

TRINIDAD, W.I. (stamped on doll's foot and neck kerchief)

About the Dolls

The authors each own a different size of this well-made cloth doll from Trinidad; photographed together the dolls make a great mother and daughter. The quality construction of these dolls is European-influenced, from the delicate pressed cloth face to the cloth over wire armature body. The facial painting is done by someone who is quite talented, and expressions vary as you can see in the photograph. The clothing is simply but nicely made, including petite cloth shoes and jewelry.

Three more examples of these Trinidad dolls can be seen in Loretta Holz's *How-To Book of International Dolls*.

Costume Description

Our pair of dolls is garbed nearly the same. Plaid three pointed turbans; gold earrings; necklace and pin; plaid short sleeved dresses with ruffles on tucked-up skirt; shoulder kerchief in solid color; white petticoat; plaid underpants and shoes. This costume is another instance of colonial influence. These dolls carry a pineapple and have Trinidad printed on the kerchief.

TURKEY

About the Doll

The look of "age" — sometimes it can really deceive us in trying to judge the date of a doll. I had assumed this fruit vendor, made of aged-looking cotton batting, was from the 1930s-40s. Imagine my surprise when, reading about the Angela Peterson Doll and Miniature Museum in High Point, North Carolina in *Dolls* magazine ("An International Gathering," Nov./Dec. 1985), I came across a photo of our peddler's twin, made in the 1960s. According to the article, Angela Peterson's "Iskenderun Peddler" was made for her by an instructor at the Ankara Art Museum in Istanbul. This proves once more how crucial it is to keep some kind of record of the dolls we buy (especially the more out-of-the-ordinary ones): where and when we bought it and who made it!

Costume Description

Fruit merchant, work clothes: small beige cap; floral print shirt; brown suit with short jacket and black shoes.

Turkish fruit vendor,
early 20th century.

10-1/2" Maker unknown Istanbul, Turkey 1960s

Cotton batting head with hand-painted features, gray cotton hair and facial hair, cloth over wire armature body

Not marked

Dnieper Area

About the Doll

Our Ukrainian girl is part of a series of ceramic-head dolls made in the Soviet Union (probably in Zagorsk) from about 1920 to the early 1930s; an example is pictured in a 1921 article in "The Mentor." Their probable precursor is the bisque-head Kämmer and Reinhardt doll in the costume of Ryazan illustrated under Russia.

Their heads were poured of thick, somewhat coarse ceramic into a Kämmer and Reinhardt mold, then painted a reddish-brown. A nearly illegible Kämmer and Reinhardt Star of David mark can still be seen on a few dolls. Their eyes are a good quality glass, but the small pupils tend to give the dolls a "staring" or startled look. Features are quite soft and blurry with very little modeling, indicating that the leftover molds they used were quite worn down.

The bodies, some stamped "Made in Russia," are a fair quality composition ball-jointed type. Like the Russian stockinet dolls that were made at the same time, their hair is a rough flax fiber, and many of the dolls wear coarsely-woven "peasant" clothing.

The author has seen at least 15 different styles of these ceramic-head dolls, all the same size: Ukraine, Smolensk, Ryazan, Veronezh, Turkestan, central Russia, and a few "boyar" costumes (wealthy Czarists in fancy gowns or heavy winter coats and hats). Other styles probably exist.

Two Ukrainian women, c.1910.

Her own little doll is a Ukrainian pincushion doll, also made in the Soviet Union, at about the same time (1920s).

Costume Description

The costumes of Kiev and Poltava are similar. Married woman in festive dress: black cotton kerchief with flowers; white cotton chemise, print trim at mid sleeve and hem; blue sleeveless jacket has a side opening and pleated lower back; blue apron trim at lower edge; red checked skirt, folded at waist to create two layers and split in front, and red boots. The floral prints imitate hand embroidery. The sash and skirt would be woven and the skirt may have red tassels on all of the lower corners.

> 12" Maker unknown (head from a Kämmer & Reinhardt mold) Russia 1920s
> Painted ceramic socket head, blue glass sleep eyes with small pupils, open mouth with teeth, gray flax hair, jointed composition body
> (Illegible Marks) // 11

Zulu people, East Natal

About the Doll

Self-help agencies are sometimes offshoots of a larger humanistic organization. The South Africa Red Cross Society, for instance, seems to have been an affiliate of the International Red Cross — well-known for its continuing aid to people in need.

For a time in the 1950s and 1960s, the South Africa Red Cross Society created these marvelous brown felt Zulu dolls. They came in several sizes up to 15", and possibly even larger. Dressed in the elaborately beaded costumes and headdresses of the Zulu people, each originally had a paper tag telling the maker and the doll's name. The tags also indicate that they were made at the Red Cross Rehabilitation Centre in Durban, South Africa.

The felt bodies are sturdily stuffed, and felt features are applied and then painted; even felt ears are applied (a feature many cloth dolls ignore). The dolls are quite beautiful and have lasted well (mind the clothes moths); definitely dolls worth looking for!

Costume Description

She has, all in beads, a headband, neckpiece, arm decor, chest piece, skirt, roll at waist, and ankle bands.

11" South Africa Red Cross Society Durban, South Africa 1950s-1960s

Felt head with applied felt features, painted nose and eyebrows, separately applied ears, black yarn wig, felt body with swing-jointed arms and legs

THE S.A. RED CROSS SOCIETY // DURBAN (paper tag, name of doll in ink on reverse)

The S.A. Red ✚ Cross Society
Durban
This is a product of the Red Cross Rehabilitation Centre. We thank you for purchasing it and hope that you and your friends will continue to support us.
H & G (DBN)

Closeup of the South African doll's label.

England
London (Pearlies)

About the Dolls

The "Pearlies," colorful street vendors of London, were so-called because of the hundreds of mother-of-pearl buttons they chose as embellishments for their costume. Every year they chose a "Pearly King" and "Pearly Queen," depicted here by Old Cottage Toys.

The Pearlies are one of the few remaining folk costumes of Great Britain, and then are found generally only in legend. But they are far more interesting to collect as dolls than the usual tourist fare depicting the semi-military, ceremonial "Beefeater" guards.

Old Cottage Toys was founded in 1948 by Margaret E. and Suzanne Fleischmann, Czech refugees from World War II. Their well-made little dolls dressed in historical, folk, and modern costumes, were sold in the better stores. The heads were made of rubber or a rubber-like material that tends to collapse if they aren't stored properly. It is still possible to find these dolls mint in their boxes, but their popularity with collectors has pushed their price up greatly in comparison to other dolls throughout this book that are equally appealing.

Costume Description

Woman in black hat and dress sewn with buttons over all; red feathers on hat, red cuffs and collar on dress.

Man in red ascot tie; black cap, jacket, and grey pants sewn with buttons all over; white shirt and leather belt.

Pearlies or costermongers of London were street traders from stands, carts or barrows selling fruits and vegetables. Monger is a trader or dealer or hawker, costard a large English variety of apple. They are associated with Cockney London East Enders. Hence the terms constermonger and barrow-boy.

8" Old Cottage Toys Sussex, England c.1970
Rubber-like swivel head with painted features, blonde mohair wig, felt body with wire armature arms
OLD // COTTAGE // TOYS // HAND MADE IN GREAT BRITAIN (paper tag) AS SELECTED FOR // THE DESIGN // CENTRE // LONDON (2nd paper tag)
Courtesy of the Rosalie Whyel Museum of Doll Art

Little boy in the "Pearly" dress of London's East End, 1920.

Scotland

About the Doll

This distinguished and jolly looking gentleman by Betsy Howard might be a portrait. He is obviously more than a bit of a caricature, with comic eyes, quite "rosy" cheeks and nose, and large, bumbling feet. Along with illustrating a folk costume, this doll is part of the larger genre of comic portraits of the period, from Mickey Mouse to Little Annie Rooney.

Costume Description

Male everyday dress, 20th century: velvet tartan tam with rabbit fur TOORIE on top, feather and pin cap ornament; shirt in white satin would more often be cotton; brown tweed jacket with gold buttons; tartan SHOULDER PLAIDE pinned with gold painted pin; blue-green tartan kilt with safety kilt pin; SPORRAN (singular) with gold painted top, lower part of rabbit fur and hair. He has white cotton undershorts, tartan hose with green garters called FLASHES, and brown leather and felt shoes with metal buckles. The tweed jacket is the clearest signal of daily dress.

He looks very like Sir Harry Lauder in character dress singing the song "When I Was Twenty-One" for which he always carried a crooked walking stick.

15" Betsy Howard Canada 1940s
Cloth head with painted features, white fur wig, jointed cloth body
BETSY HOWARD ORIGINAL (paper tag glued to skirt)
Courtesy of the Rosalie Whyel Museum of Doll Art

Romantic Victorian depiction
of a Scotsman.

Scotland

About the Doll

The Kämmer and Reinhardt mold #115 character doll called "Phillip," beloved by doll collectors, wears his original Scottish regalia. He may have been dressed by the factory — straight out of a book on costume, because the Victorian-style costume is earlier than the period of the doll. Or he may have been dressed in Scotland for a special occasion. The tartan plaids and kilts of Scotland — especially the fanciful dress of the male, with the haunting strains of a bagpipe in the distance — have always seemed to inspire doll makers and other artists.

Costume Description

Male costume in the 19th century Romantic style: On his head is a Glengarry (a style of hat) trimmed in tartan; white shirt with collar; black jacket with silver buttons; tartan SHOULDER PLAIDE; tartan kilt; he is missing his SPORRAN; short tartan boots. Tartan hose and black shoes with silver buckles would be traditional.

In 1746 after the Battle of Culloden, all Highland clothes were forbidden until 1782 when the law was repealed. The growing romance with tartans and all things Scottish was accelerated in 1822 with the visit of King George IV to Scotland. His successful sojourn was guided by Sir Walter Scott.

The Scottish male costume is divided into several forms, some of which are daily dress, formal dress, dance costume, and military wear; none of these have remained static over the years.

16" Kämmer & Reinhardt
Waltershausen, Germany c.1912

Bisque socket head, brown glass sleep eyes, closed mouth, brown mohair wig, ball-jointed composition toddler-style body

V // K * R // S & H // 115A // 38

Courtesy of the Rosalie Whyel Museum of Doll Art

Wales

About the Doll

A papier-mâché doll from the 1840s or '50s, in such pristine condition that one might believe that the doll, Welsh costume, and peddler notions are all from the same period. However, a closer look reveals that a large number of the items that she peddles are from a later date. It was especially popular in England in Victorian times, and later, to create peddler dolls. They often used older dolls which, of course, were far more plentiful then!

Costume Description

Peddler, working attire: frilled lace cap tied under the chin; tall black hat; white blouse; red checked turned-back, split-front over-dress; red and black striped gathered skirt; black and white checked apron; large red wrap. All major garments in a rough local wool. A shoulder shawl is usually worn and an enveloping red cape with hood may be worn. Mostly hidden by the red wrap is her baby's red and white dotted dress.

10–1/2" Maker unknown Germany c.1840s
Papier-mâché shoulder head, painted features, painted black hair, unjointed kid leather body with wooden lower arms and legs
Not marked

Welsh woman in her traditional tall
hat, early 20th century.

African-American

About the Dolls (pages 161-162)

We cannot begin to address the subject of African-American dolls adequately here, but their clothing is certainly a part of the folk costume history of the United States. Our earlier doll, probably made in Germany in the first few decades of the 20th century, is dressed as a so-called black "mammy" doll. This red-and-white-checked, kerchiefed and white-aproned image of the southern black slave woman persisted long after slavery was abolished. The image was "stuck" for decades in popular culture, its main perpetuator being the warm and friendly "Aunt Jemima."

Contemporary African-Americans have searched for their roots in Africa, often identifying themselves with the continent through a creative jumbling of African cultures in fabrics, hairstyles, jewelry and costume elements. Certainly our modern doll (on the next page) by Uta Brauser, a German woman living in New York, depicts this "Africanized" urban dweller.

Two German doll portraits of African-Americans, less than a hundred years apart, show us how well dolls can reflect radical change in a culture's history.

Costume Description

Red and white checked dress, ruffle at neck and flounce at hem; white gathered apron with eyelet border. This costume, which reflects an earlier time period, may have a turban and a neckerchief or fichu. The colors and prints are frequently checks or polka dots, but florals were also worn. The turban, fichu, and apron were often of crisp white cotton.

14" Maker unknown Germany c.1920s
Composition head with inset glass eyes, black curly mohair wig, cloth body with composition lower arms and legs
Not marked
Courtesy of the Rosalie Whyel Museum of Doll Art

* **Photograph of second doll representing an African-American appears on page 162.**

African-American

Costume Description

Girl in modern play outfit reflecting pride of ancestry. Pillbox hat; white shirt; red over shirt; jumpsuit in West African stripweave print and molded colorful "canvas" shoes.

21" Uta Brauser
Germany 1993

Bisque swivel head on shoulder plate, painted features, black synthetic hair in multiple braids, cloth body and upper limbs over wire armature, bisque lower limbs, molded and painted shoes

U (MONOGRAM) // UTA.

Native American Eastern Woodlands

About the Dolls

Called the "Scowling Indian" mold by doll collectors due to their very stern faces (they can be dramatically unhappy in larger sizes), these dolls can be found in a variety of Native American costumes. Most of the dolls are in fringed and beaded leather, because that is what Europeans came up with when they tried to picture the American Indian. The quality of the bisque on these dolls varies greatly.

This pair wears Eastern Woodlands type clothing, which does not seem to be distinctive to a particular tribe. They are of reasonably good quality, although the wire "stringing" of the heads does not allow for much posing — the dolls remain with their noses stuck in the air. The workmanship of the dolls, their wigs and their clothing is quite high for this late period of German mass-marketed dolls.

Costume Description

Both dolls have hair in two braids. He wears a blue felt vest; black felt jacket with brown fringe on sleeves and yellow embroidery; red pants with brown fringe down the sides; yellow sash.

She has plastic beads; red wool dress with blue and grey embroidery; brown and beige striped blanket wrapped around body. These costumes have been simplified, perhaps by time and distance from the true subject matter.

11-1/2" Armand Marseille Koppelsdorf, Germany c.1925
Bisque socket head, inset brown glass eyes, open mouth with teeth (so-called "Scowling Indian"), black mohair wig, ball-jointed composition body
4 / 0

Native American Hopi, Shoshonean of Pueblo Indians

About the Doll

Barton Wright's excellent book *Hopi Kachinas: The Complete Guide to Collecting Kachina Dolls* offers a detailed story of these unique dolls. It is recommended reading for anyone interested in the subject, and I have referred to it in developing a brief synopsis.

Kachinas are spirits within the Hopi religion, personifying all important aspects of life. A ritual opening of the underground ceremonial chambers, or "kivas," in late December allows the kachinas to come and go until the end of July. Three main ceremonies throughout this period involve them, symbolically represented by men dancing in kachina masks. Some dancers were traditionally also carvers, who created replicas of their kachinas for the children and women. These were not playtoys, but hung in sacred places throughout the home.

Visitors to the Hopis have demanded, since the earliest times, to buy these kachina "dolls," eventually creating a demand for them that far outstripped the carvers' production and exhausted local supplies of the root of the cottonwood tree. Attempts were made to mass-produce the dolls (with mostly awful results). Changes in paints occurred, from the old clay-based ones to tempera paints and finally to acrylic. Action pose kachinas came about in the 1960s due to increased interest in greater realism.

The wolf kachina, known in Hopi as the "kweo" kachina, is a side dancer who accompanies other animal kachinas such as the deer and mountain sheep. At the end of a dance, he is offered a meal and prayer feathers, so that the Hopi might also be good hunters.

Dating from the 1960s, this wolf kachina is transitional between older and newer styles. He is carved in a stylized action pose, nowhere near as elaborate as today's dolls. His sharp teeth, fangs and tongue show the development of greater realism. And he is painted with tempera or poster paints (which tend to rub off easily), a method which went out of style with the introduction of acrylic paints in the late 1960s.

Costume Description

Wolf kachina: leather, fur, paint, and cloth create his costume. He wears mask, body paint, loin cloth, and moccasins. He is holding a bow and arrow.

10" LeRoy Kenejestewa Arizona, United States 1964

Painted wooden wolf-shaped head, painted brown eyes, open mouth with carved teeth, 4 front fangs, feather hair, carved wooden one piece body with added tail

Not marked

Courtesy of the Rosalie Whyel Museum of Doll Art

Native American Navajo

About the Dolls

Navajo dolls are some of the best-known and recognized Native American dolls. The dolls have been made for tourists in the same manner for many years: cloth dolls with painted or embroidered features, simple bodies with little or no jointing of the limbs, and emphasis on the costumes and the famous "silver" jewelry.

This classic Navajo pair is similar to one illustrated in Janet Pagter Johl's 1941 book *The Fascinating Story of Dolls*. This helps to date the dolls which, because of their fine condition, were initially dated in the 1950s or even 1960s! This is not to say that the doll maker could not have made similar dolls later than 1941, but often their style changed or the quality declined.

This pair is neatly made, and all of the printed fabric and simplified (not silver) jewelry is nicely crafted to scale. Their cloth faces are simply but sweetly painted. Perhaps someone who has a pair of dolls by this presently unknown maker can tell us who made them.

Costume Description

Man has a headband tied to one side; bead earrings; purple velvet tunic shirt lined in purple cotton print; sequins used as shirt buttons; bead necklace; cloth and metal belt; black sateen pants; short cloth boots.

Woman wears bead necklace and earrings; purple velvet tunic blouse; metal concho buttons; red cloth belt with metal disks; full green print skirt with red trim; wrapped legs and red cloth short boots and cotton print petticoat.

The colors and prints may vary but cut and type of garments will remain the same. This woman's dress developed in the late 19th century and derives from fashionable dress of the time.

> 7-1/2" Maker unknown (Native American, Navajo) United States 1940s
>
> Cloth head with hand-drawn ink features, black floss and cloth wig, cloth body with swing-jointed limbs
>
> Not marked

Native American Navajo people, c.1940s.

State of Florida
Native American
Seminole, Muskhogean
Indians

About the Doll

The resemblance of this Seminole tribe doll to the construction of the popular "Skookum Indian" dolls designed by Mary McAboy is remarkable. The reason for the similarity is unknown, but we can guess that an enterprising doll maker "borrowed" the idea of the Skookum wooden body and stick legs wrapped in cloth, plus the rectangular flat feet, and added this very uniquely-modeled composition head. Skookum dolls had blankets wrapped around in such a way as to indicate crossed arms; this doll doesn't, but Seminole dolls traditionally do not have arms anyway.

"Traditional" Seminole dolls have heads, and sometimes conical bodies, made of palm fiber. Their colorful, distinctive costumes are very similar to that of our composition-head doll. Modern Seminole dolls have fewer bands of colored fabric, but have added rows of contrasting colored bias tape or rickrack. We've included a close-up of actual Seminole "patchwork" fabric here.

The unusual black cloth half-circle "hat" of Seminole dolls is actually the female hairstyle. You can see this distinctive "do" quite well on the doll shown here!

Costume Description

Everyday dress: Hair would be worn in a special pompadour; multiple beads around the neck; blouse and skirt made of patchwork in bright colors; narrow purple underskirt; beige footwear.

M-89   HIPTENEA OSCEOLA AND BABY CONAPATCHEE, SEMINOLE CHILDREN,

IN THE FLORIDA EVERGLADES, NEAR MIAMI

Young Seminole girl
and her little brother,
U.S., 1940s.

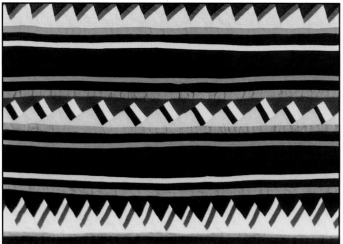

Opposite page:

13-1/2" Maker unknown (Native American, Seminole)
United States 1950s-1960s

Cloth head with hand-drawn ink features, black floss and cloth wig, cloth body with swing-jointed limbs

Not marked

Seminole machine-sewn
patchwork fragment,
U.S., late 20th century.

State of Alaska Native American Iñupiat people (Eskimo)

4"—12" Ethel Washington (Eskimo) Kotzebue, Alaska, United States 1960s

Wooden swivel head with carved and inked features, fur hair, hide body with swing-jointed limbs

Not marked

Courtesy of the Rosalie Whyel Museum of Doll Art

About the Dolls

Ethel Washington, whose native name was *Agnauglugaq*, was born on May 1, 1889 near Kotzebue, Alaska. Her parents were Isaac Marley and Mary Lincoln. Missionaries liked to give native peoples of Alaska "Christian names" honoring famous Americans; for instance, one of Ethel Lincoln's brothers was named Abraham. The interesting salute to American presidents continued when Ethel Lincoln married a young native man named George Washington.

Ethel and George Washington had eleven (possibly thirteen) children, born from 1906 to 1928. Sadly, many of them died by the 1930s from tuberculosis, polio, or tragic accidents. By the time George became too old and ill to hunt in 1937, Ethel was faced with a need to help support them. She turned her skin-sewing skills to making Eskimo dolls.

Ethel was a very small, shy but jolly woman who liked to make people laugh. She sat on the floor with her legs out straight in front of her — as was her custom — carving her heads and sewing scraps of furs. People who knew her said she often took "cat naps," putting her head in her lap and snoozing away in that stretched-out sitting position!

Ethel died in October, 1967. Her dolls, never made in large number, have become collector's items. With their expressive wooden heads and intricately-sewn hide and fur clothing, they are amongst the finest Eskimo dolls ever created.

For more on the life and dolls of this fascinating woman, see *Ethel Washington: The Life and Times of an Eskimo Doll Maker* by co-author Susan Hedrick and her husband Basil.

Costume Description

The family wears similar garments of hooded parka, pants, and boots, all in fur and hide. A great variety of furs are used for an artistic result.

State of Wyoming Native American Shoshoni

6"—10" Wanda Moon (Shoshone Indian) Wind River Reservation, Wyoming, United States 1965

Hide head with embroidered features, black human hair, soft hide body, not jointed

Not marked

Mercedes Gardner collection

About the Dolls

Jane and Sarah Gregory, keepers of this wonderful family of Shoshone Indian dolls, received them from a friend in 1991. The family of dolls was ordered in early 1965 from Wanda Moon, who lives on the Wind River Reservation in Wyoming. But they were not received until very late in the year. Wanda Moon explained that the men had killed no deer that year, preventing her from making the dolls when they were ordered.

Males and children or babies are usually much harder dolls to find in traditional costume, so it is nice to have a family such as this one. The baby is snuggled in her cradleboard, a method used by some indigenous mothers to carry their young. Other cultures use baby straps, or other methods. All of these methods are fair game to lots of beading and other ornamentation.

The Shoshone comprise a major group among what are commonly known as the Plains Indians. The use of beaded and fringed tanned animal hide is a common element among many of the dolls made by the Plains Indians.

Costume Description

His hair in three braids; a fringed buckskin shirt; blue wool loin cloth; fringed pants and beaded moccasins.

She has two long braids; buckskin fringed and beaded dress; ornamental beaded belt, pocket and soft boots. They share many characteristics with other Plains Indians.

State of Hawaii

14-1/2" Patty Kanaar and Peggy Hinshaw (Hei Mana Creations) Van Nuys, California, United States 1994

Poured cold-cast resin shoulder head with painted brown eyes, closed mouth, black mohair wig, cloth torso and upper limbs, poured resin lower arms and legs

KANAAR//(c)'91 '94 (head) ISLAND TRADITIONS-THIS CARD CERTIFIES THAT THIS IS AN ORIGINAL DOLL BY PATTY KANAAR (tag) HULA KAHIKO(c)// GREEN & WHITE/ 1994// PATTY KANAAR (inside tag, left doll) HULA KAHIKO// PURPLE//#34/500 1994//PATTY KANAAR (right doll)

Diana Honda and Mindi Reid collections

About the Dolls

Patty Kanaar has been making Polynesian dolls for about four years, according to Ariel Zeitlin's article, "A Taste of Polynesia" (*Dolls,* January 1995). Patty and her mother, Peggy Hinshaw, form the doll-making company "Hei Mana" (Tahitian for "sacred crown"). Both women work at sculpting, constructing the dolls, costuming them and marketing them. They make a mold in plastylene (a type of clay) and then mold the dolls in cold-cast resin, adding upper limbs of cloth over wire.

Neither Patty Kanaar nor her mother are Polynesian, but they spent much time on the islands on location with her motion picture

director and producer father. Patty and her husband are both involved in traditional Polynesian dance. Patty explains: "It's not my culture, but I admire it so much. This is my way of being part of it." (Zeitlin, *ibid.*)

Costume Description

"Hula Kahiko": For our two Polynesian women, flowers constitute their jewelry; floral wreath over flowing hair; floral lei and green ti leaves; peasant style long sleeved blouses; gathered skirts; overskirt with stenciled border or grass; both carrying gourd instruments.

Virgin Islands

11" Virgin Islands Native Products
Virgin Islands c.1940 (Male),
1958 (Female)

Cloth head with embroidered features,
black wool wig, cloth body with
swing-jointed arms and legs

HANDMADE BY NATIVES
IN THE VIRGIN ISLANDS OF
THE UNITED STATES OF
AMERICA FOR THE
COOPERATIVES. STOCK NO. A-4
(paper tag on male) (LOGO) //
VIRGIN ISLANDS NATIVE
PRODUCTS (reverse of tag)

About the Dolls

The authors are quite partial to this Virgin Islands pair with embroidered faces and nifty vintage clothing (notice his very wide tie and blue bead watch chain). They are the type of doll that makes a collection of 20th century folk dolls so fascinating and, well, so much fun.

The Kimport catalog of 1936 (and subsequent years) shows a pair of 12" Virgin Island dolls which includes our gentleman. This lady was purchased later, in 1958, but shows so little change from the Kimport illustration that she was no doubt made by the same island industry, Virgin Islands Native Products, or by its successor.

Costume Description

His wardrobe consists of a colorful straw hat; green and white plaid shirt; large red and white dotted tie; blue tie pin and blue bead watch chain; brown striped pants; his shoes match the hat.

Her apparel includes a plaid turban with three points; dress with leg-of-mutton sleeves in white printed cotton; plaid neckerchief; earrings and necklace; patchwork apron; pink straw shoes; white petticoat and pantalets; straw carry bag. The style of garments will be the same however the colors and prints may vary widely.

URUGUAY

12" Maker unknown (Methodist missionary) Montevideo, Uruguay 1943

Head with oil-painted face and features, black floss hair, cloth body with swing-jointed limbs, mitten hands

Not marked

Courtesy of the Rosalie Whyel Museum of Doll Art

About the Doll

Fearn Brown, author of *The Dolls of the United Nations*, illustrates this pair of dolls which eventually made their way, via Jane and Sarah Gregory, to the Rosalie Whyel Museum. Brown reports that they were made for her in 1943 by one of the Methodist Hatfield groups, a missionary group akin to the Wesleyan Service Guild in Montevideo.

The artist who skillfully and artfully painted these dolls was quite obviously an accomplished portrait painter. She (or perhaps he) treated the flat cloth surfaces of their faces like a canvas, creating human visages so lifelike and three-dimensional that you expect this gaucho and lady from Uruguay to walk out of the picture. Compare these dolls to the ones from Argentina; if Kimport thought "Ricardo from Argentina" could steal all the lady's hearts, what would they have said about this handsome devil from Uruguay!

Costume Description

Her hair in two braids and a red ribbon around her head; white silk neckerchief; floral print dress, ruffle at the elbow and hem; white cotton apron and red felt shoes.

Man's Gaucho Sunday dress: white silk is the fabric of his headband, neckerchief, and shirt. Cotton would be more common. A black wool vest; white, lace edged underdrawers; black silk wrap pants called CHIRIPA (singular) (again a heavy cotton or wool would be more usual), and boots to finish. He may wear a black felt hat and a wide ornamental leather belt.

These costumes are European influenced and are very similar to Gaucho dress in Argentina and parts of Brazil.

UZBEKISTAN

About the Doll

There are "sleepers" in doll collecting still, and a few great bargains to be had. I believe (as I discuss in more detail in the introduction), that some of the cloth dolls featured in this book are to be had for a song right now, but it probably won't stay that way forever. Many of the dolls are plentiful at the moment, but more and more people are discovering them, and succumbing to their many charms.

I stumbled onto this pair from southern Asia — possibly two of the rarest dolls in this book, in a shoebox under a dealer's table at a doll show (for the lowest price I have paid for two dolls in ages!). The vendor specialized in an entirely different type of dolls, and these were just not of interest. But to the authors, who had been desperately searching for a doll — any doll of quality, from the little-known countries (Uzbekistan or Tajikistan, for instance) created by the break-up of the former Soviet Union, this was the "find" of the book! And they are delightful, unusual dolls — to make our "fairytale" complete!

Costume Description

Ordinary female dress: orange chiffon veil; metal earrings; red crepe tunic with black print indicating the wonderful resist fabrics called IKAT. Full pants with gold braid trim; she would wear an embroidered pillbox hat. The woman on the left, wearing her hair in braids, open sleeve tunic, gathered skirt and small pillbox hat, is from either Turkmenia or Tajikistan. Both frequently wear an embroidered vest over the tunic.

12" Maker unknown Uzbekistan c.1950s-1960s
Pressed cloth head with painted features, black yarn hair in four braids, cloth body with swing-jointed arms and legs
Not marked

Dancers of Uzbekistan, mid 20th century.

Sumadija Region, Serbia

About the Doll

Gebrüder Heubach of Lichte, Germany in Thuringia had the special ability, in their figurines and dolls, to capture a child's innocence and roguish charm. Delightful dolls — laughing, grinning proudly with their two front teeth, pouting or even crying — these were perfect to costume as little children from anywhere in the world.

A young Serbian fellow by Heubach, from days before the Balkan conflicts became everyday news, wears a wonderful costume no doubt created in his homeland. His intricately-woven stockings and exact miniature replicas of the high-laced, curled-toe shoes unique to this region are beautifully made. Again, it is so nice to find dolls like this in their original regional costumes. Hopefully, we will begin to learn more about where the costumes are from and the cultures that they represent.

Costume Description

Man's summer costume: conical fur hat; long white shirt with red embroidery on collar and cuffs; blue vest with braid trims; hand-woven sash wrapped around the waist; full white pants tucked into multicolored knit stockings; handmade sandals called OPANKI (plural). Extremely turned-up toes distinguish Serbian OPANKI.

15-1/2" Gebrüder Heubach Lichte, Germany c.1912
Bisque socket head with painted blue intaglio eyes, open mouth with two teeth, molded hair, ball-jointed composition body
3 // GERMANY

YUGOSLAVIA
Sumadija Region, Serbia

About the Dolls

Kimport began to import this superb little line of dolls, available in two small sizes (5" & 8"), from the former Yugoslavia in the spring of 1957. There is also a scarce 12-1/2" size, which was probably not widely imported to the U.S. Kimport continued to sell the dolls in the early 1970s; other companies such as Mark Farmer also featured them in their catalogs. The dolls were distributed by a Yugoslavian folk arts cooperative called Narodna Radinost ("folk arts"); some dolls are found with a tag from this company.

Each stockinet face has hand-embroidered features and hand-applied and styled floss or mohair wigs. Delicate and well-proportioned bodies are fashioned of cloth over wire armatures, with simple flat hands of felt.

The costumes are just as fine and minutely-scaled, utilizing lovely small weavings and multicolored hand-embroidery, small cotton laces and soft wool felt. They are some of the nicest dolls in folk costume offered to collectors in latter years. Do not overlook them!

Costume Description

Festive attire: fur hat; white full sleeved shirt embroidered on collar, cuffs, and front; vest and pants can be in black or brown wool; woven red sash and bag; black stockings and Serbian sandals called OPANKI (plural). Vest may be heavily braided, and stockings for both male and female are frequently embroidered with flowers. The jodhpur-like pants are the result of military contact during World War I.

Festive wear: hair is worn braided and wrapped around head with flowers at the side; white chemise with open sleeve and neck frill, embroidered on front and lower sleeve, and red ribbons tie the sleeve. The felt bodice, imitating velvet, is mostly in dark colors such as black, navy blue, and dark red, embroidered in gold or silver thread. Hand-woven red sash should have ends hanging more to the side. Lace edged apron embroidered in flowers; an earlier style was woven. The hand-woven pleated skirt can be worn in different ways as shown. The tucked-up version is named the butterfly skirt. Black stockings and Serbian OPANKI (plural) are worn.

8" Maker unknown, distributed by Narodna Radinost Belgrad, Yugoslavia 1950s-1970s

Stockinet head with embroidered features, floss wig (doll on left has mohair wig), cloth body over wire armature, felt hands

Not marked

Jaye Delbridge collection (male doll)

Shona people

15" Maker unknown
Zimbabwe 1980s

Lozenge-shaped mask head of woven fiber, molded and painted features, brown fiber "hair", woven fiber body kneeling with outstretched arms, not jointed

Not marked

Courtesy of the Rosalie Whyel Museum of Doll Art

About the Doll

Masked dolls can be quite fascinating to collect; you can find examples from many countries all over the world. Some of the most visually exciting, and certainly the most unusual, come from Africa. In the strictest sense, they are not international costume dolls, but our criteria have never been strict in putting this book together — just that the dolls be interesting. And that the wild masked dancer from Zimbabwe certainly is!

His huge, lozenge-shaped head mask, formed of a woven and blue-stained fiber and graphically painted in red and white, rather resembles a monkey or baboon in its decoration. Brown fiber fringe hangs like a curtain over his upper body and arms. His whole kneeling body and wildly-gesturing arms are shaped from the plaited blue fiber and striped boldly with red and white. A skirt formed of the brown fiber seems to bring balance to the whole piece.

More examples of these interesting masked dancers from Zimbabwe are shown in Polly and Pam Judd's *African and Asian Costumed Dolls*.

Costume Description

Ritual dance costume: On his head is a diamond-shaped mask. A blue painted body suit and a hemp fringed skirt form the rest of his attire.

BIBLIOGRAPHY (DOLLS)

Compiled by Susan Hedrick.

BOOKS:

Anderton, Johana Gast. *The Collector's Encyclopedia of Cloth Dolls.* Wallace Homestead. Lombard, Illinois, 1984.

Argyriadi, Maria. *Dolls in Greek Life and Art from Antiquity to the Present Day.* Lucy Braggiotti Publications. Athens, 1991.

Art Education Museum of Toys. *Russian Folk Toys.* USSR Academy of Pedagogical Sciences, Zagorsk, Russia, n.d.

Axe, John. *Collectible Dolls in National Costume.* Hobby House Press. Riverdale, MD, 1977.

Bofinger, Ilse. *Puppen aus fünf Kontinenten.* Battenberg Verlag. Augsburg, Germany, n.d.

Brown, Fearn. *The Dolls of the United Nations.* Vantage Press. New York, 1965.

Buhler, Edith E. *Dolls Around the World.* Crosby House, Oklahoma City, 1946.

Chauveau, Elisabeth. *Poupées et Bébés en Celluloid (1881-1979).* Centre d'Etudes et de Recherche sur la Poupée. Paris, 1991.

Cieslik, Jürgen and Marianne. *German Doll Encyclopedia 1800-1939.* Hobby House Press. Cumberland, Maryland, 1985.

Cole, Adeline P. *Notes on the Collection of Dolls and Figurines at the Wenham Museum.* Wenham Historical Society. Wenham, MA, 1951.

Coleman, Dorothy S., Elizabeth A. and Evelyn J. *The Collector's Encyclopedia of Dolls.* Crown Publishers. New York, 1968.

————. *The Collector's Encyclopedia of Dolls Volume Two.* Crown Publishers. New York, 1986.

Fainges, Marjory. *The Encyclopedia of Australian Dolls.* Kangaroo Press. Kenthurst, Australia, 1993.

————. *The Encyclopedia of Regional Dolls of the World.* Kangaroo Press. Kenthurst, Australia, 1994.

Foulke, Jan. *Simon & Halbig Dolls, The Artful Aspect.* Hobby House Press. Cumberland, MD, 1984.

Frame, Linda Jean. *Folk and Foreign Costume Dolls: An Identification and Value Guide.* Collector Books. Paducah, Kentucky, 1980.

Gordon, Lesley. *A Pageant of Dolls.* A.A. Wyn, Inc. New York, 1949.

Gribben, Jill and David. *Japanese Antique Dolls.* Weatherhill. New York, 1984.

Hallen, Julienne. *How to Make Foreign Dolls and their Costumes.* Homecrafts. New York, 1950.

Hansmann, Claus. *Puppen Aus Aller Welt.* Verlag F. Bruckman. Munich, 1957.

Hart, Luella. *Dolls Tell the Story of Brittany.* Privately published, 1956.

Hedrick, Basil and Susan Pickel-Hedrick. *Ethel Washington: The Life and Times of an Eskimo Doll Maker.* Alaska Historical Commission Studies in History No. 31. Alaska Historical Commission. Anchorage, 1983.

Hillier, Mary, ed. *Pollock's Dictionary of English Dolls.* Crown Publishers. New York, 1982.

Holz, Loretta. *The How-To Book of International Dolls.* Crown Publishers. New York, 1980.

Hooper, Elizabeth. *Dolls the World Over.* n.p. Baltimore, 1939.

Johl, Janet Pagter. *The Fascinating Story of Dolls.* H.L. Lindquist Publications. New York, 1941.

————. *Your Dolls and Mine.* H.L. Lindquist Publications. New York, 1952.

Johnson, Judi. *Native American Dolls and Cradleboards.* Illinois State Museum Handbook of Collections No. 4. Illinois State Museum. Springfield, 1983.

Jones, Suzi, ed. *Eskimo Dolls.* Alaska State Council on the Arts. Anchorage, 1982.

Jordan, Nina R. *Homemade Dolls in Foreign Dress.* Harcourt, Brace & World, Inc. New York, 1939.

Judd, Polly and Pam. *European Costumed Dolls.* Hobby House Press. Grantsville, MD, 1994.

————. *African and Asian Costumed Dolls.* Hobby House Press. Grantsville, MD, 1995.

Koenig, Marie. *Poupées et Legendes de France.* Librairie Centrale des Beaux-Arts. Paris, 1900.

McQuisten, Don and Debra. *Dolls and Toys of Native America.* Chronicle Books. San Francisco, 1995.

Nolan, Helen. *Lenci Dolls in Full Color.* Dover Publications. New York, 1986.

Porot, Ann Marie and Jacque, and Francois Theimer. *S.F.B.J.: Captivating Character Children.* Hobby House Press. Cumberland, MD, 1986.

Poupée-Jouet, Poupée-Reflet. Exhibition catalog. Muséum National d'Histoire Naturelle. Paris, 1983.

Schoonmaker, Patricia. *Research on Kämmer and Reinhardt Dolls.* n.p. 1965.

Singleton, Esther. *Dolls.* (Reprint of 1927 edition). Hobby House Press. Washington, D.C., 1962.

Stohl, Walter. *Trachtenpuppen aus Hessen.* Museum catalog. Hessischer Museumsverband. Kassel, Germany, 1977.

Theimer, François. *The Bru Book.* Theriault's Gold Horse Publishing. Annapolis, MD, 1991.

White, Gwen. *Dolls of the World.* Mills and Boon. London, 1962.

Wright, Barton. *The Complete Guide to Collecting Kachinas.* Northland Publishing. Flagstaff, AZ, 1977.

Yamada, Tokubei. *Japanese Dolls.* Japan Travel Bureau. Tokyo, 1955.

MAGAZINES AND NEWSPAPERS:

Baten, Lea. "Delicate Treasures of Japan." *Dolls.* May 1955. pp. 80-82.

"Brazilian Dolls." *London Studio.* October 1943. p.131.

Buchmann, Mary Lou. "Dolls in Regional Costumes of Western Europe." *Doll Reader®.* May 1986, pp. 190-195.

Campbell, Lorraine. "Sweden's Charlotte Weibull." *Doll Reader®.* October 1983. pp. 180-182.

Chiara, Joan. "Foreign Dolls." *Hobbies.* November 1975. pp. 39-40.

"Chinese Play Dolls." *The Doll World.* December 1956-March 1957. p. 10.

Coleman, Dorothy S. "Regional Costume Dolls." *Doll Reader®.* April-May 1981. p. 94.

Coleman, Dorothy S. and Evelyn Jane. "McKim Studios and Kimport in the 1930s." *Doll Reader®* June/July 1992. pp. 98-102.

————. "Poupées du Litoral." *Spinning Wheel.* April 1976, pp. 21-23.

————. "Twentieth-Century Russian Rarities." *Dolls.* January 1994. pp. 66-69.

DeFeo, Barbara. "Norwegian Heritage: The Enchanting Dolls of Ronnaug Petterssen." *Antique Doll World.* November 12, 1994. pp. 57-62.

"Dolls of All Nations." *The Mentor.* December 1, 1921. pp. 32-33.

"Dolls of All Nations—As An International Hobby." *Christian Science Monitor.* December 26, 1935. p. 8.

"Dolls of the Month [Ingeborg Neilsen dolls]." *Hobbies.* June 1941. No pag. cit.

Fields, Mary Durland. "An International Gathering." *Dolls.* November/December 1985. pp. 42-44.

Goff, Diane M. "João Perotti Cloth Dolls." *Doll Reader®* February 1994. pp. 58-59.

Groninger, Margaret. "20th Century Russian Dolls." *Living Dolls and Miniatures.* 1980, p. 16.

————. "Wee Immigrants: Latin American Dolls." *Doll News.* Summer 1986. pp. 64-67.

————. "Wee Immigrants: Part I." *Doll News.* Summer 1983. pp. 68-72.

Hathaway, Mary. "Around the World with Dolls." *National Doll World.* March/April 1984, pp. 45-46.

————. "Around the World with Dolls: Austria." *National Doll World.* November/December 1982. pp. 37-39.

"Icelandic Dolls." Advertisement for Krug Doll House. *House Beautiful.* December 1941. No pag. cit.

Judd, Pam and Polly. "The Forever Fashionable Province Dolls of France." *National Doll World.* November/December 1984. pp.38-42.

Knüsli, Laura. "Swiss Wooden Dolls from Brienz." *Doll Reader®* February 1995. pp.66-69.

Law, Margaret. "Dolls—Internationally Speaking." *The Independent.* December 17, 1927. pp. 602.

Lewis, Peggy. "The Norwegian Dolls of Ronnaug Petterssen." *Doll News.* Summer 1990. pp. 21-23.

Pickering, Barbara. "Chinese Nodders." *Doll Reader®* July 1987. pp. 62-64.

————. "Dolls from Kenya." *Doll Life.* April 1994. pp.56-57, 67.

————. "From Far Away Places." *Doll and Toy World.* August 1986. pp. 31-33.

————. "Handcrafted Dolls from Ethiopia." *National Doll World.* July/August 1987. pp. 35-56.

————. "Introduction Into Collecting Ethnic Costume Dolls." *National Doll World.* January/February 1990. pp. 69-72.

————. "Ronnaug Petterssen—A Norwegian Felt Doll Artist." *Doll Reader®* May 1988. pp. 189-191.

Planton, Patricia Sullivan. "The Door of Hope Reopened." *Doll Reader®* February/March 1980. pp. 12-13.

Sefton, Joyce. "Shanghai Treasures: Door of Hope Dolls." *Doll Reader®* February 1996. pp. 66-70.

Smith, Gini. "Of Lands and Dolls." *Doll Castle News.* July/August 1980. pp. 53-54.

Smith, Marjorie R. "Old Cottage Toys." *Doll Reader®* June/July 1985. pp. 92-93.

Spaulding, Judith. "Dolls in Scottish Costume." *Doll Reader®* August/September 1990. pp. 187-191.

Theimer, François. "French Regional Costumes as seen through the Doll." *Polichinelle.* pp. 45-49.

Wellman, Loraine. "The Dolls of Thailand (Part I)." *Doll Reader®* October 1992. pp. 124-127.

Yeshi, Kim. "Preserving Tibetan Traditions (Part I)." *Dolls.* July/August 1989. pp. 94-98.

————. "Preserving Tibetan Traditions (Part II)." *Dolls.* September/October 1989. pp. 50-53.

Zeitlin, Ariel. "A Taste of Polynesia." *Dolls.* January 1995. pp. 79-80.

OTHER:

Brown, Fearn. Cataloging notes from personal collection. c.1940. ms.

Gregory, Jane Everest. Cataloging notes from personal collection. n.d. ms.

————. "Know Your Foreign Costume Dolls: An Identification Guide—Eastern European Countries." 1978. ms.

Kimport Dolls. "Foreign Folk Dolls." Catalog. Independence, Missouri. 1936-1940 (later issues become part of "Doll Talk").

————. "Doll Talk." Newsletters. Independence, Missouri. 1938-1984.

Krug, Elsie Clark—International Doll House. Newsletters. Baltimore, MD. March 1, 1941 - August/September 1955.

Le Minor. "Les Poupées de Bretagne." Company catalog. Pont L'Abbe, France. c.1939.

Mark Farmer Co. "Catalog of Dolls." Company catalogs. El Cerrito, CA. c.1957-c.1972.

"Die Volkskunst." Brochure of Czechoslovakian folk art. Germany(?). c.1960s.

Weibull, Charlotte. Company brochure. Akarp, Sweden. n.d.

World-Wide Doll Club. Brochure. Greenvale, N.Y. 1950s.

BIBLIOGRAPHY (COSTUME)

Compiled by Vilma Matchette with David Clelland.

GENERAL WORKS:

Alford, Violet ed. *Handbooks of European National Dances.* Max Parrish and Company. London, 1950s.

Akahira, Kakuzo. *Festivals and Costumes in the World.* George Allen & Unwin, Inc. Tokyo, 1971.

Baizerman, Suzanne, Joanne B. Eicher and Catherine A. Cerny. *Ethnic Dress: An Exploration of Terminology with Implications for Research Teaching.* The Costume Society of America 15th Annual Meeting and Symposium: Ethnic Dress: Origins and Influences. Denver, 1989.

Basilov, Vladimir N. ed. *Nomads of Eurasia.* Natural History Museum of Los Angeles County in association with University of Washington Press. Seattle and London, 1989.

Bradshaw, Angela. *World Costume.* Macmillan Co. New York, 1953.

Braun and Schneider. *Historic Costume In Pictures.* Dover Publications, Inc. New York, 1975.

Bruhn, Wolfgang and Max Tilke. *A Pictorial History of Costume.* Praeger, New York, 1955.

Burnham, Dorothy. *Cut My Cote.* The Royal Ontario Museum. Ontario, 1973.

Durham, M. R. *Some Tribal Origins, Laws, and Customs of the Balkans.* George Allen & Unwin Ltd. London, 1928.

Evans, A. M. *Costume Throughout The Ages.* J. B. Lippincott Co. Philadelphia, 1938.

Fairservis, Walter A. Jr. *Costumes of the East.* American Museum of Natural History, Chatham Press. Connecticut, 1971.

Fox, Lilla M. *Folk Costume of Western Europe.* Chatto, Boyd & Oliver, 1969 and Plays Inc. Great Britain, 1971.

Gerlach, Martin, ed. *Primitive and Folk Jewelry.* Dover Publications, Inc. New York, 1971.

Gervers, Veronika. "The Influence of Ottoman Turkish Textiles and Costume in Eastern Europe." *History, Technology, and Art.* Monograph 4. Royal Ontario Museum. Toronto, 1982.

Gostelow, Mary. *Embroidery: Traditional Designs, Techniques, and Patterns from All Over the World.* Marshall Cavendish Editions. London, 1977.

Grolier. *Land and Peoples Vol. I: British Isles and Western Europe.* Grolier Inc. New York, 1963 (original publication: 1929).

Halouze, Edouard. *Costumes of South America.* New York, 1941.

Harold, Robert and Legg, Phyllida. *Blandford Colour Series: Folk Costumes of the World.* Blandford Press, Poole, Dorset, 1978.

Hecht, Ann. *The Art of the Loom: Weaving, Spinning, and Dyeing Across the World.* Rizzoli, New York, 1989.

Holme, Charles Geoffrey and A. F. Kendrick. *A Book of Old Embroidery.* The Studio, Ltd. New York, 1921.

Kennett, Frances. *Ethnic Dress.* Reed International Books. New York, 1995 (first printed in Great Britain by Mitchell Beazley, an imprint of Reed Consumer Books Ltd., 1994).

Larsen, Jack Lenor. *The Dyer's Art: Ikat, Batik, Plangi.* Van Nostrand Reinhold. New York, 1976.

Mann, Kathleen (notes by J. A. Corbin). *Peasant Costume in Europe.* A. & C. Black, Ltd. Soho, London, 1935.

Meilach, Dona Z. *Ethnic Jewelry.* Crown Publishers. New York, 1981.

Oakes, Alma and Margot Hamilton Hill. *Rural Costume.* Van Norstrand Co. Batsford, London and New York, 1970.

Paine, Sheila. *Embroidered Textiles: Traditional Patterns from Five Continents.* Rizzoli International Publications, Inc. New York, 1990.

Racinet, Albert. *The Historical Encyclopedia of Costume.* Best Seller Publications Ltd. London, 1991 (Originally printed in France by Racinet in 6 volumes entitled *Le Costume Historique* between 1876 and 1888.).

Silverstein, Mira. *International Needlework Designs.* Charles Scribner's and Sons. New York, 1978.

Snowden, James. *European Folk Dress.* Costume Society of England, V. & A. Museum. London, 1973.

————. *The Folk Dress of Europe.* Mayflower Books, Inc. New York, 1979.

Tilke, Max. *National Costumes from East Europe, Africa, and Asia.* Hastings House Publishers, Inc. New York, 1978.

———. *Costume Patterns and Designs.* Hastings House Publishers, Inc. New York, 1974.

———. *The Costumes of Eastern Europe.* Ernest Benn, Ltd. London, 1926.

———. *Oriental Costumes.* Paul, Trench, Trubner. London, 1923.

Webster. *Webster's New Geographical Dictionary.* Merriam-Webster. Springfield, Massachusetts, 1988.

Yarwood, Doreen. *The Encyclopedia of World Costume.* Bonanza Books. New York, 1986.

SPECIFIC WORKS:

Adams, Frank, revised by Innes of Learney. *The Clans, Septs, and Regiments of the Scottish Highlands.* W. & A. K. Johnston, Ltd. London, 1952.

And, Metin. "Dances of Anatolian Turkey." *Dance Perspectives:* Summer 1959.

Anderson, Ellen. *Danish Folk Costumes.* Gyldendalske Boghandel Nordisk Forlag. Copenhagen, 1948.

———. *Folk Costumes in Denmark.* Hassing Publisher, Copenhagen, 1952.

Andrejic, Ljubomir. *Bibliografija o narodnoj nosnji jugoslovenskih naroda.* (Bibliography of the Folk Dress of the Yugoslav People). Ethnografski Muzej. Beograd, 1976.

Balassa, Ivan and Gyula Ortutay. *Hungarian Ethnography and Folklore.* Corvina Press. Budapest, 1979.

Banateanu, Tancred, Gheorghe Focsa and Emilia Ionescu. *Folk Art in the Rumanian Peoples Republic.* Costumes-Woven Textiles-Embroideries. State Publishing House for Literature and the Arts. Bucharest, 1958.

Baud-Bovy, Daniel. *Peasant Art in Switzerland.* The Studio, Ltd. London, 1924.

Benaki, Antony E., ed. *Hellenic National Costume.* Benaki Museum. Athens, 1954.

Berg, Inga Arno and Gunnel Hazelius Berg. *Folk Costume of Sweden.* Ica Bokforlag Vasteras. Sweden, 1985.

Binder, Pearl. *The Pearlies; A Social Record.* Juniper Books. London, 1975.

Bing, M. "The Crafts of the Puszta." *Ciba Review:* Number 45. Basle, Switerland, March 1943.

Bjeladinovic, Jasna. *Narodne Nosnje Jugoslavije.* (Folk Costumes of Yugoslavia). Etnografski Muzej. Beograd, 1976.

Blackard, David M. *Patchwork and Palmettos: Seminole-Miccosukee Folk Art Since 1820.* Fort Lauderdale Historical Society. Fort Lauderdale, Florida, 1990.

Brandon, Reiko Mochinaga. *Country Textiles of Japan: The Art of Tsutsugaki.* Weather Hill. New York and Tokyo, 1986.

Burrow, T. *Decorative Arts of the New Zealand Maori.* Wellington & Auckland. Reed Publishers, 1964.

Calderini, Emma. *Il Costume Popolare in Italia.* Sperling & Kupfer. Milan, 1946.

Campbell, Margaret and Nakorn Pongnoi. *From the Hands of the Hills.* Media Transasia. Hong Kong, 1978.

Coe, Ralph. *Lost and Found Traditions.* University of Washington Press. Seattle.

Conn, Richard. *Robes of White Shell and Sunrise: Personal Decorative Arts of the Native American.* Denver Art Museum. Denver, November 1974-January 1975.

Cordry, Donald Bush and Dorothy. *Mexican Indian Costumes.* University of Texas Press. Austin and London, 1961, 1968.

Covarrubias, Luis. *Mexican Native Costumes.* Ed. Fischgrund Publisher. Mexico

———. *Mexican Native Dances.* Ed. Fischgrund Publisher. Mexico.

Covarrubias, Miguel. *Mexico South: The Isthmus of Tehuantepec.* Cassell and Company, Ltd. London.

Crowfoot, Grace M. and Phyllis M. Sutton. "Ramallah Embroidery". *Embroidery.* Volume III, Number 2, March 1935, pp 25-39.

Creston, R. Y. *Les Costumes Des Populations Bretonnes.* Generalites, Volume I. Rennes, 1953; La Cornovaille, Volume II. Rennes, 1954.

Cyr, Georges. *Lebanese and Syrian Costumes.* Imprimerie Catholique. Beirut.

Dannenberg, Linda. "Souleiador: The Spirit of Provence." *Connoisseur.* Volume 221, Number 847, September 1982.

De Giafferri, P. L. *Costumes Regionaux.* Librarie Grund. Paris, April 1955.

De Palencia, Isabel. *El Traje Regional de España.* Voluntad. Madrid, 1926.

De Vries, R. W. P. *Beautiful Holland: Dutch National Costumes.* J. M. Meulenhoff. Amsterdam.

Dean & Carell. *Dust For The Dancers*. Philosophical Library. New York, 1955.

Dmytriw, Olya, compiler. *Ukrainian Arts*. Ukrainian Youth's League of North America Inc. New York, 1952.

Dongerkery, Kamala S. *The Indian Sari*. The All India Handicrafts Board. New Delhi.

Echague, José Ortíz. *España Tipos y Trajes*. Ortiz Echague. Madrid or Bilbão, 1957.

Eicher, Joanne Bubloz. *African Dress: A Selected and Annotated Bibliography of Subsaharan Countries*. African Studies Center, Department of Textiles, Clothing and Related Arts, Michigan State University. East Lansing, December 1969, 1973.

Etnoloski Muzej. *Makedonski narodni nosii* (Les Costumes Nationaux en Macedoine or The National Dresses of Macedonia). Etnoloski muzej. Skopje, 1963.

Fairservis, Walter. *Costumes of the East.* The Chatham Press, Inc., Published in association with the American Museum of Natural History. Riverside, Conn., 1971.

Feder, Norman. "The Side Fold Dress." *American Indian Art Magazine*. Volume 10, Number 1, Winter 1984, Page 48.

Florescu, Elena. *Portul Popular Din Zona Neami Din Cultura Traditionala A Judetului Neamt.* Series # 1 (Folk Costume of the People in the Cultural Tradition of the District of Neamt). Comitetul de Cultura si Educatie Socialista al Judetului Neami. Bucharest, 1979.

Fochler, Rudolf. *Costumes in Austria*. Welsermuhl Wels-München. Munich, 1965.

Formagiu, Hedvig Maria. *Portul Popular Din Romania: catalog tipologic*. Muzuel de arta populara al Republicii Socialiste Romania (Popular Art Museum of the Socialist Republic of Romania). Bucharest (Bucuresti), 1975.

Gaborjan, Alice. *Hungarian Folk Art 3: Hungarian Peasant Costumes*. Kossuth Printing House. Corvina, 1969.

Gallois, Emile. *Costumes Des Provinces Françaises*. H. Laurens-Paris ed. Paris.

Gamble, David. *The Wolof of Senegambia: Ethnographic Survey of Africa, Western Africa Part XIV.* International African Institute. London, 1976.

Gattuso, John, ed. *Insite Guides: Native America*. APA Publications (HK.) Ltd., 1991.

Gervers-Molnar, Veronika. *The Hungarian Szur: An Archaic Mantle of Eurasian Origin*. History, Technology, and Art Monograph 1, Royal Ontario Museum. Toronto, November 23, 1973.

Gjergji, Andromaqi. *Veshjet Shqiptare ne Shekuj*. Instituti I Kultures Popullore. Tirane, 1988.

Gilfoy, Peggy Stoltz. *Patterns of Life: West African Strip-weaving Traditional*. Smithsonian Institution Press for the National Museum of African Art. Washington, D. C., 1987.

Gómez, José M. *Tesoro del Folklore Español*. Editorial Tesoro Ediciones Segl. XX. Madrid, 1950.

Grounds, Cynthia Tso. "Navajo Women's Dress as Associated with Navajo History from 1860 to 1910." *Ethnic Dress: Origins and Influences*. The Costume Society of America, 15th Annual Meeting and Symposium. Denver, May 1989.

Gurzau, Elba Farabegoli. *Folk Dances, Costumes, and Customs of Italy*. Folkraft Press. Newark, 1964.

Gusic, Marijana. *Commentary on the Exhibited Material*. Ethnographic Museum Zagreb. Zabreb, 1955.

————. *Folklor Naroda Jugoslavije*. (Folklore of the People of Yugoslavia). Grafickog Zavoda Hrvatske. Zabreb, 1963.

Hasalova, Vera and Jaroslav Vajdis. *Folk Art of Czechoslovakia*. Arco Publishing Company, Inc. New York, 1974.

Hart, Luella. *Dolls Tell The Story of Brittany*. Oakland, 1956.

Hartman, Sheryl. *Indian Clothing of the Great Lakes: 1740-1840*. Eagle's View Publishing Company. Liberty, Utah, 1980s.

Hatzimichali, Angeliki. *The Greek Folk Costume: Costumes With The Sigouni*. Volume II. Trans. Diana Dalkafouki-Reid. "Melissa" Publishing House. Athens, 1984.

Hayashi, Tadiachi. *Japanese Women's Folk Costumes*. Ie-No-Hikari Association. Tokyo, 1960.

Hijlkema, Riet. *National Costumes in Holland*. J. M. Meulenhoff. Amsterdam, 1951.

Holme, Charles, ed. *Peasant Art In Austria and Hungary*. The Studio, Ltd. London, Paris, and New York, 1911.

————. *Peasant Art In Italy*. The Studio, Ltd. London, Paris, and New York, 1913.

————. *Peasant Art In Russia*. The Studio, Ltd. London, 1912.

————. *Peasant Art In Sweden, Lapland and Iceland*. London, 1910.

————. *Peasant Art In Switzerland*. The Studio Press. London, 1924.

Johnstone, Pauline. *A Guide to Greek Island Embroidery*. Victoria and Albert Museum, Her Majesty's Stationery Office. London, 1972.

Jouglet, Rene. *Mazawsze Chants et Danses Du Folklore Polonais.* Cahiers Du Cercle D'Art, 1954.

Kalapesi, Roshan, compiler. *Sringar: A Pageant of Indian Costume.* Air India Collection.

Kalashnikove, Natalia and Galina Pluzhnikov. *National Costumes of the Soviet Peoples.* Planeta Publications. Moscow, 1990.

Kawakatsu, Ken-Ichi. *Tourist Library Volume 3: Kimono.* Japan Travel Bureau, Tokyo, 1954.

Keatinge, Margaret Clark. *Costumes of the Holy Lands.* Margaret Keatinge Clark, publisher. Beirut, 1957.

———. *Costumes of the Levant.* Khayats College Book Coop. Beirut.

Keim, Anne. *The Costumes of France.* French and European Publications Incorporated. New York, 1929(?).

Kent, Kate P. *Introducing West African Cloth.* Denver Museum of Natural History. Denver, 1971.

Keohane, Alan. *The Berbers of Morocco.* Hamish Hamilton, Ltd. London, 1991.

Kirin, Vladimir. *Narodne nosnje Jugoslavije: Bosna I Hercegovina, Crna Gora, Hrvatska, Makedonija, Slovenija, Srbija, Kosovo, Vojvodina.* (The Folk Costume of Yugoslavia: Bosnia and Hercegovina, Montenegro, Croatia, Macedonia, Slovenia, Serbia, Kosovo, Vojvodina). Zagreb: Nasa Djeca, 1986.

Koch, Ronald P. *Dress of the Plains Indians.* University of Oklahoma Press. Norman & London, 1932, reprinted 1977.

Koev, Ivan. *Bulgarskata Vezbena Ornamentika: prinos kum istoriiata na narodnii ornament* (Bulgarian Embroidered Ornament) Izdanic na Bulgarskata Akademiia na naukite, (Bulgarian Academy of Sciences). Sofia, 1971.

Kundig, W. and H. Wescher. "Roumanian Peasant Textiles." *Ciba Review.* 60, 1947.

Lanuza, José Luis. *The Gaucho.* MacDonald-London. London, 1968.

Lauder, Sir Harry. *Roamin' In The Gloamin'.* Lippincott. London and Philadelphia, 1928.

Lebar, Frank M., Hicey, and Musgrave. *Ethnic Groups of Mainland South East Asia.* Human Relations Area Files Press. New Haven, 1964.

Leis, A. "Turkestan and Its Textile Crafts." *Ciba Review.* Number 40, August 1941.

Lepage-Medvey-A. Varagnac. *National Costumes of Austria, Hungary, Poland and Czecho-Slovakia.* Hyperion Press. Paris, 1939.

Lewis, Paul and Elaine. *People of the Golden Triangle.* Thames and Hudson. London, 1984.

Luching, Wolf. *Trachtenleben in Deutschland-III: Hessen.* Akademie-Verlag-Berlin. Berlin, 1959.

Majka, Christopher and Sheilagh Hunt. *Polish Folk Costumes.* Empty Mirrors Press. Halifax, Nova Scotia, Canada, 1991.

Manga, Janos. *Herdsmen's Art in Hungary.* Corvina Press. Budapest, 1972.

Manker, Ernst and Tre Tryckare. *People of Eight Seasons.* Crescent Books. New York, 1972.

Markov, Jozef. *The Slovak National Dress Through the Centuries.* Artia. Prague, 1956.

Martin, Pat, compiler. *Czechoslovak Culture.* Penfield Press. Monticello, Iowa, 1989.

McIan, R. R. *The Clans of the Scottish Highlands: The Costumes of Clans.* Crescent Books. New York, 1985 (first published in 1845 and 1847).

Minnich, Helen Benton and Shojiro Nomura. *Japanese Costume and the Makers of Its Elegant Tradition.* Charles E. Tuttle Company. Rutland, VT and Tokyo, 1963.

Monchaux, Marie-Claude. *Le Costume Breton.* Rennes, Editions Ouest-France. France, 1994.

Murphy, E. Jefferson. *Understanding Africa.* T. Y. Crowell Company. New York, 1969.

Naslednikova, Venera. *(A) History of Bulgarian Costume.* Nouka i izkustro. Sofia, 1974.

Nylein, Anna Maja. *Swedish Peasant Costumes.* Nordiska Museet. Stockholm, 1949.

Onassis, Jacqueline, ed. with the cooperation of The Metropolitan Museum of Art. *In The Russian Style.* A Studio Book, The Viking Press. New York, 1976.

Oprescu, George. *Peasant Art in Roumania.* The Studio Press. London, 1929.

Oy, Helmi Vuorelma. *Finnish National Dresses.* Julkaisja. Lahti, Finland, 1987.

Papantoniou, Ioanna. "A First Attempt at an Introduction to Greek Traditional Costume (Women's)." *Ethnographica.* Volume 1, 1978, pp. 5-92.

Payne, F. G. *Welsh Peasant Costume.* National Museum of Wales, Welsh Folk Museum. Cardiff, 1969.

Pendergrast, Mick. *Te Aho Tapu, The Sacred Thread: Traditional Maori Weaving.* University of Hawaii. Honolulu, 1987.

Pesendorfer, Gertrud. *Lebendige Tracht in Tirol.* Universitatsverlag Wagner. Innsbruck, 1966.

Petrakis, Joan. *The Needle Arts of Greece: Designs and Techniques.* Charles Scribner's Sons. New York, 1977.

Petterson, Carmen. *The Maya of Guatemala: Their Life and Dress.* Ixchel Museum. Guatemala City, 1972.

Pettigrew, Dora W. *Peasant Costume of the Black Forest.* A. & C. Black, Ltd. Soho, London, 1937.

Primmer, Kathleen. *Scandinavian Peasant Costume.* Adam and Charles Black. London, 1939.

Rajab, Jehan. *Palestinian Costume.* Kegan Paul International. London and New York, 1989.

Rehm, Maria. *Österreichs Trachtenbuchlein.* Austrian National Costumes, 1954.

Reklaff, Hans. *Deutsche Bauerntrachten.* Ut. Berlag. Berlin, 1934.

Ross, Heather Colyer. *The Art of Arabian Costume: A Saudi Arabian Profile.* Arabesque. Fribourg, 1981 (Second Edition 1985).

Rubens, Alfred. *A History of Jewish Costume.* Funk and Wagnalls. New York, 1967.

Rugh, Andrea B. *Reveal and Conceal: Dress in Contemporary Egypt.* Syracuse University Press. New York, 1986.

Sayer, Chloe. *Mexican Costume.* British Museum Publications. London, 1985.

Scott, A. C. *Chinese Costume in Transition.* Donald Moore, Publisher. Singapore, 1958.

Secosan, Elena, Paul Petrescu and Nina Stanculescu. *Portul Popular De Sarbatoare Din Romania. Folk Costume from Holiday in Romania.* Editura Meridiane. Bucharest, 1984.

Shaver, Ruth M. *Kabuki Costume.* Charles E. Tuttle Company. Rutland and Tokyo, 1966.

Sieber, Roy. *African Textiles and Decorative Arts.* The Museum of Modern Art. New York, 1972.

Skavhaug, Kjersti and Bent Vanberg. *Norwegian Bunads.* Hjemmenes Forlag. Oslo, Norway, 1982.

Solheim II, Wilhelm G., Father Gabriel Casal, Regaldo Troto Jose Jr., Eric S. Casino, and George R. Ellis. *The People and Art of the Philippines.* Museum of Cultural History, University of California. Los Angeles, 1981.

Southby, Susan. *Costumes of the Holy Land.* Susan Southby, publisher. Beirut, 1957.

Souza, Alberto. *O Trajo Popular Em Portugal Nos Seculos XVVIII E XIX.* Socio Efectivo Da Associacão dos Arqueologos Portugueses. Lisboa (Lisbon), 1937.

Spencer, Mrs. Phyllis. *Panama y su Folklore.* Inter-American Women's Club. Colon, 1948.

Stalder, Valerie. *Lapland: Journey By Reindeer Sledge.* This Beautiful World Series Volume 26, Kodansha International, Ltd. Tokyo and Palo Alto, 1971.

Start, Laura F. *Bankfield Museum Notes: The Durham Collection of Garments and Embroideries From Albania and Yugoslavia.* Bankfield Museum Notes, Third Series Number 4. The Halifax Corporation. Halifax, 1939; Calderdale Museums, 1977.

Stillman, Yedida Kalfon. *Palestinian Costume and Jewelry.* University of New Mexico Press. Albuquerque, 1979.

Stone, Caroline. *The Embroidery of North Africa.* Longman. Harrow, Essex, 1985.

Swanton, John R. *The Indian Tribes of North America.* Smithsonian Institution, Government Printing Office. Washington, D.C., 1953.

Toor, Frances. *Festivals and Folkways of Italy.* Crown Publishing Incorporated. New York, 1953.

———. *A Treasury of Mexican Folkways.* Crown Publishers. New York, Third Printing, 1950.

Tyrchniewicz, Peggy. *Ethnic Folk Costumes In Canada.* Hyperion Press Ltd. Winnipeg, Canada, 1979.

Tyrell, Barbara. *Suspicion Is My Name.* Cape Town, 1971.

———. *Tribal Peoples of Southern Africa.* Books of Africa. Cape Town, 1971.

Undi, Maria. *Hungarian Fancy Needlework and Weaving.* Stephaneum Press. Budapest, 1930s.

Vaclavik, Antonin and Jaroslav Orel. *Textile Folk Art.* Spring Books. London.

Van Hemert, Maria. *The Needlework of the Island of Marken.* National Folk Museum "The Netherlands Open-Air Museum". Arnheim, Netherlands, 1978.

Van Thienen, F. W. S. and J. Duyveter. *Klederdrachten: De Schoonheid Van Ons Land.* Uitgeverij Contact. Amsterdam, 1962.

Veleva, Maria. *Bulgarian National Attire* (color plates). Czechoslovakia, 1950.

———. *Bulgarian Folk Costumes.* Tamburitza Press. Pittsburg, 1982.

Veleva, Maria and E. L. Lepavtsova. *Bulgarian Folk Costumes of Central West Bulgaria and the Central West Rhodopes in the 19th and the First Half of the 20th Centuries.* Volume II (Bulgarski Narodni Nosii) Bulgarian Academy of Sciences. Sofia, 1974.

————. *Bulgarian Folk Costumes of North Bulgaria in the 19th and Early 20th Centuries.* Volume I (Bulgarski Nosnii) Publishing House of the Bulgarian Academy of Sciences. Sofia, 1974.

Veleva, Maria and V. Venedikova. *Tissus Et Techniques De Tissage Dans La Bulgarie Du Sud-Est Du Nord-Ouest* (Fabrics and Techniques of Fabrics in the Bulgaria of the South-east and North-west). Regions: Sliven, Yambol, Kotel, Vidin, Kula. Editions de L'Academie Bulgare des Sciences. Sofia, 1967.

Vincent, John Martin (1857-1939). *Costume and Conduct in the Laws of Basel, Bern and Zurich 1370-1880.* Greenwood Press. New York, 1969.

Von Hammerstein, Hans (wrote forward). *Trachten der Alpenlander im Herbert Reichner Verlag.* Wien (Vienna), Leipzig, and Zurich, 1937.

Weir, Shelagh. *Palestinian Embroidery.* British Museum. London, 1970.

Welters, Linda. *Women's Traditional Costume in Attica Greece.* Peloponnesian Folklore Foundation. Athens, 1988.

Zimmerman, Robert. *Enchantment of the World: The Gambia.* Children's Press. Chicago, 1994.

Zunic-Bas, Leposava. *Folk Traditions in Yugoslavia: Ten Tours.* Trans. Karin Radovanovic. Izdavacki Zavod Jugoslavija. Beograd, 1966.

OTHER SPECIFIC WORKS:

African Textiles and Decorative Arts. Museum of Modern Art. New York, 1972.

Costumes et Coutumes. Revue De La Federation Nationale des Costumes Suisses. 15 annee, No. 2, AOUT 1942; 19 annee, No. 2/3, AOUT 1946.

Decorative Folk Art of the Ukraine S.S.R. State Museum of Ukraine, 1968.

Etnografia Shqiptare (Ethnograph of the Shiptars) Akademia e Shkencave e RPS TE Shqiperise. Institute of Culture Populaire. Tirana, Number IX 1980, Number 11—1981, Number 13—1982, Number 14—1983, Number 15—1987.

Exhibition of Paintings by Cesareo Bernaldo De Quirós: Gaucho Life in Argentina (Province of Entre Rios) 1850-1870. The Hispanic Society of America. New York, 1932.

Exhibition of Polish Folk Art. Polish Cultural Institute. London.

Indians of the Americas. National Geographic Society. Washington, D.C., 1955.

Narodne nosnje Jugoslavije: Dalmacija, Bosna, Hercegovina. (The Folk Costume of Yugoslavia: Dalmatia, Bosnia, Hercegovina). I. Zagreb: Nasa Djeca, 1954-1958.

Narodne nosnje Jugoslavije: Srbija, Makedonija, Crna Gora, Vojvodina. (The Folk Costume of Yugoslavia: Serbia, Macedonia, Montenegro, Vojvodina). II. Zagreb: Nasa Djeca, 1954-1958.

Narodne nosnje Jugoslavije: Hrvatska. (The Folk Costume of Yugoslavia: Croatia). III. Zagreb: Nasa Djeca, 1954-1958.

Narodne nosnje Jugoslavije: Slovenija, Istra, Hrvatsko Primorje. (The Folk Costume of Yugoslavia: Slovenia, Istria, Croatian Plains). IV. Zagreb: Nasa Djeca, 1954-1958.

The Near East in U.C.L.A. Collections. Museum and Laboratories of Ethnic Arts and Technology (University of California, Los Angeles), 1969.

Palms and Pomegranates: Traditional Dress of South Arabia. U.S. Committee for Saudi Arabian Cultural Heritage (exhibit). Washington, D.C., 1987-1989.

Polski Stroj Ludowy. Muzeum Archeologiczne I Etnograficzne W Lodzi, Katalog Wystawy. Lodz, 1983.

Russian Embroidery. Traditional Motifs (Russian with English). The Museum of Folk Art. Sovetskya Russiya Publishers. Moscow, 1990.

Swiss Peasant Costumes. Ciba Review: Number 55. Basle, Switzerland, February 1947.

Traditional Embroidery Portugal. Anchor Embroidery Book 1, B. T. Batsford, Ltd. London.

COSTUME GLOSSARY

Compiled by Vilma Matchette.

Many of these words and terms have alternate spellings and meanings, as in Sop, Shope, and Schope. In a great number of cases, the words have been transliterated from another alphabet, such as Cyrillic. It is not uncommon to have three or four different interpretations of a word because transliterations are not uniform. The terms for particular garments are frequently localized. There is no consistency upon which we can depend.

Bast: a strong woody plant fiber used in Russia to make footwear.

Bandolier: a belt worn over the shoulder and across the chest, often to support a bag, or as part of ceremonial dress.

Batintawk (singular): from the Philippines — female country-style costume.

Betzel (singular): from Schwalm, Germany — a small cylindrical hat.

Bodice (singular): female — laced corset reaching from waist to bust.

Bourgoin (singular): from France, female — tall starched lace coif.

Bragon Bas: from Brittany, France, male — wide pleated pants.

Brekusha (singular): from Albania, male — baggy semi-wide pants.

Bum Roll (singular): padded hip roll or bolster originating in the 16th and 17th Centuries.

Bunad (singular): from Norway, male and female — a recreated folk costume based on well researched prototypes.

Chadri (singular): from Afghanistan, female — all enveloping outdoor garment.

Chemise: female — basic undergarment which is visible at the neck, chest, sleeves, and hem.

Chiripi (singular): from Uruguay, male — wrap pants worn in Argentina and Uruguay.

Choli (singular): from India, female — cropped close fitting blouse.

Ciocie: from Italy, male and female — simple hide sandal.

Csikos (plural): from Hungary — herdsmen of the plains.

Derby (singular): male — dome shaped felt hat with narrow brim.

El Muntuno (singular): from Panama, male — embroidered two piece costume.

Faldetta (singular): from Azores, Portugal, female — hooded full length cape.

Fedora (singular): male — low felt hat with medium brim and creased crown.

Fez (singular): male — felt cone shaped hat worn by Muslims.

Fichu (singular): female — scarf or shawl draped around the shoulders and tied in front or back of the body.

Flashes (plural): from Scotland — ribbons attached to garters.

Foustanella (singular): from Greece, male — a pleated lower body garment worn in mainland Greece and Albania.

Gallardete (singular): from Panama, female — bright colored ribbons that fall from the waist of the skirt.

Gatya (singular): from Hungary, male — very wide pants.

Geisha (singular): from Japan — girl trained to provide entertainment, usually for men.

Ghoutra (singular): from Saudi Arabia, male — traditional head wrap. Called Kaffiyeh elsewhere.

Gjurdin (singular): from Albania, male — short sleeved jacket of wool.

Glengarry (singular): from Scotland, male — style of wool cap with creased crown.

Gumbag (singular): from Saudi Arabia, male — an over robe.

Halsmantel (singular): from Germany, female — separate yoke which goes over the shoulders and is attached to the bodice.

Hennin (singular): female — high headdress of various shapes and sizes originating in the 15th Century.

Huaraches (plural): from Mexico, male and female — sandal made from leather strips.

Huik (singular): female — hooded cape worn in the Azores and Malta, originating in North Africa; worn through much of Europe in the 15th Century.

Huipil (singular): from Mexico, female — an indigenous, square cut, upper body garment of various lengths.

Igaal (singular): from Saudi Arabia, male — band to hold kerchief on the head.

Ikat : from Indonesia — resist fabric dyed in the warp threads before weaving. Known elsewhere by other names.

Jodhpur (singular): male and female — riding breeches, full above the knee and narrow below.

Kierpce (plural): from Poland, male and female — simple hide shoes.

Kimono (singular): from Japan, male and female — unfitted loose robe with wide sleeves.

Klompen (plural): from Netherlands, male and female — heavy wooden shoes.

Koto Missie (singular): from Surinam, female — dress derived from missionary attire.

Kotula (singular): from Croatia, female — a continuously pleated skirt. Also called krilo.

Kraplap (singular): from Netherlands, female — winged garment which rolls over the shoulders and ties on with strings.

Kukeri (plural): from Bulgaria, male — springtime ritual dancers.

Lapa (singular): Spreewald, Germany, female — stiffened and embroidered lace edged headdress.

La Montuna (singular): from Panama, female — country costume worn in Ocu and Las Tablas, called the man killer.

La Pollera (singular): from Panama, female — elegant embroidered costume.

Leg-of-Mutton: style of sleeve, full at the top with fitted lower arm popular in the mid 19th Century.

Litham (singular): head wrap and face veil, covering head, nose, mouth and neck, worn by Taureg men and Muslim women.

Marama (singular): from Romania, female — oblong head veil.

Mate (singular): from South America — an aromatic beverage, likened to tea.

Mintan (singular): from Albania, male — under jacket or vest.

Mocassin (singular): Native American, male and female — soft leather footwear.

Mule (singular): backless slipper.

Obi (singular): from Japan, female and male — traditional sash worn over kimonos.

Opanki (plural): from Yugoslavia, male and female — native footwear made of strips of leather.

Parka (singular): Inuit, male and female — hooded tunic.

Partlet (singular): female — detachable yoke covering neck and shoulders.

Pinner Apron (singular): female — an apron that is pinned to the costume.

Plaide (singular): from Scotland, male or female — rectangular tartan fabric worn over the shoulder.

Plastron (singular): female — separate front piece of woman's dress going from chest to waist, usually ornamental.

Pokamiso (singular): from Greece, female — chemise.

Pompons (plural): male or female — decorative wool or silk ball used on caps and clothing.

Puszta (singular): from Hungary — great plain.

Rebozo (singular): from Mexico, female — long rectangular multipurpose stole or shawl.

Resist Textiles: fabrics treated with wax, mud, or rice paste to resist dyes, such as batik.

Rubac (singular): from Moravia, female — pleated skirt.

Sari (singular): from India, female — a rectangular length of fabric draped to form a skirt and shawl or veil.

Scapulaires (plural): from Brittany, France, female — a pair of decorative squares hanging from the shoulder and falling onto the breast.

Schlappe (singular): from Switzerland, female — headdress on small cap supporting an ornamental lace halo.

Serape (Sarape) (singular): from Mexico, male — blanket-like garment worn as a cloak or poncho.

Shayla (singular): from Saudi Arabia, female — long scarf or stole.

Sirwaal (singular): from Saudi Arabia, male or female — under pantaloons. Also known as chalvar, chalwar, and salvar.

Skaut (singular): from Norway, female — starched kerchief headdress for married women.

Skirt-Pocket (singular): from Scandinavian countries and Portugal, female — decorative pocket worn at the hip, tied at the waist with tapes.

Sobre-Pantalones: from Guatemala, male — decorated over-pants taken from Spanish prototypes.

Soukman (singular): from Bulgaria, female — sleeveless dress worn over a chemise.

Sporran (singular): from Scotland, male — a pouch or purse made of skins or leather worn center front of kilt.

Szur (singular): from Hungary, male — traditional great coat.

Tabi: from Japan, male and female — fitted socks fastened at the ankles.

Tarboosh (singular): hat similar to the fez worn by Muslim men.

Templeques (plural): from Panama, female — decorative hair ornaments made of silver wires, pearls, and sequins worn over La Pollera costume.

Thawb (singular): from Saudi Arabia, male and female — all enveloping robe.

Tiki (singular): from New Zealand, Maori — image of God or spirit of the Creator of mankind in Polynesian myth.

Toorie (singular): from Scotland, male and female — pompon on a cap such as the glengarry and the balmoral.

Torque (singular): usually rigid collar or necklace open on one side. Was also worn in Antiquity.

Tovaglia (singular): from Italy, female — folded headdress, usually white.

Tsaroukia: from Greece, male and female — black or red leather footwear usually with large woolen pompons on the toes.

Tunic (singular): male or female — unfitted over garment, knee length or longer, sometimes belted.

Uchikake (singular): from Japan, female — loose unfitted jacket worn over the kimono.

Vilnic (singular): from Romania, female — pleated open wrap skirt.

Vraka (singular): from Greece, male — baggy island pants, to the knee or longer.

Zori: from Japan, male or female — sandal made of cloth and straw.

INDEX

A

Ada Lum 22
Adolf Thomann...............................147
Aebeltoft 33
AFGHANISTAN 7
African-American 16, 161-162
Agemaki 83
Akha Group 151-152
Alaska (Native American Inupiat, Eskimo) 168
ALBANIA.....................................8, 58
Alberani Vecchiotti 79
Alburquerque 137
Alexandra Kukinova 125
ALGERIA...9
Algonquian 20
Alice Barrutia-Wynn...........................62
Allina, Zygmunt K........................5, 118
Alpine 80
Alps-Maritimes Department 38-39
Alsace Region..........................5, 41, 50
Amdo...25
Andalucia Region 134
Anderson, Ellen 33
Andhara Pradesh State 70
Andreas Voit 57
Anna Fehrle....................................53
Appenzell Canton 148
Arab Refugee Handworks Centre................87
Aran Islands 75
Arango, Senior, Don Francisco.................63
Arctic Circle 37
ARGENTINA 10, 16, 172
Armand Marseille......29, 49, 56, 99, 101, 109, 163
Arouani Brothers 149-150
Attica 58-59
Attica and Boeotia Departments.................58
AUSTRALIA 11, 112
AUSTRIA 12-13
Azores 120

B

Badajoz Province 137
Baden State 53
Bahia 15-16
Baitz Dolls 148
Balkans 8
Bani Tamim...................................130
Barbara Pickering..............................23
Baronne Sandra Belling 5, 149-150
Barrois, Eugene-Constant...................13, 131
Barrutia-Wynn, Alice 62
Bas-Rhin & Haut-Rhin Departments 41
Batik 73
Batintawak 114
Bedouin.......................................149
BELGIUM 14
Belling, Baronne Sandra 5, 149-150

Berber People 97
Bernard Ravca.................................149
Berne Canton.......................5, 146-147
Betsy Howard 158
Betzel 51
Bistritza-Nasaud District.......................121
Black Forest.................................53-55
Bohemia 30
Bohemian Forest..............................30
Borsod County 66-67
Bourg-de-Batz.................................45
Bourgoin.......................................48
Bragon Bas 45
Brandenburg Province.........................56
Bratina-Kupinec................................28
Brauser, Uta 161-162
BRAZIL....................10, 15-16, 172
Brekusha 8
Brittany Region 5, 43, 45-47
Brown, Fearn 27, 64
Bru Jne. et Cie............49, 82, 131-132
Buddhist 25
BULGARIA.................................17-18
Bullock's Dolls from Many Lands 118
Bum Roll 101
Bunad 109
BURMA 151
"Busy Bees" Girl's Club.......................49

C

CAMBODIA....................................89
CANADA 19-21
Cannes 38-39
Caribbean 34
Carmen Miranda 16, 94
Carpathian Mountains.........................118
Caserta..78
Catholics 41, 103
Cavanova, Maria 32
Cepelia Union of Handicraft And
   Folk Art Cooperatives.....................116
Chadri 7
Charlotte Weibull..........................144-145
Charro 94
CHINA....................22-25, 151
China Poblana 94
Chiripa.......................................172
Chodsko 30
Choli 70-71
Christa Seva Mandir Doll Production Circle 70
Chubba 25
Chupa 25
Cicmany 133
Ciocie 76
Cockney 157
COLOMBIA....................................26
Compania Compartimento 78

Coop Arta Crisana.............................121
COSTA RICA 27
Costermongers 157
Costume Society of America 4
Cottbus 56
County Donegal 75
Courtesan 83
Crèche (Nativity) Figures 78
Cree, Native Canadian 20
CROATIA 28-29
Csikos 68
Culloden 159
Cuzco 113
CZECH REPUBLIC 30-32
Czechoslovakia (See *SLOVAKIA &*
   CZECH REPUBLIC)........................133

D

Dalecarlia Region 143
Dalmatia 29
Debar..92
DENMARK 5, 33
Dickinson, Velvalee 33, 98
Dnieper Area 155
Dogue, Sandra, Les Poupées 93
Dolfi 101
Dolls of the United Nations 27, 64
DOMINICA 34
don Francisco Arango, Senior 63
Donegal, County 75
Door of Hope Mission 24
Doudleby......................................30
Dovina Company 102
Druse 149-150
Dunham, Katherine...........................16
Durgin 150

E

East Funin Island 33
East Natal 156
Eastern Cree 2, 6, 20
Eastern Woodlands 163
Edo Period....................................83
Eisenhower, Dwight 134
El Montuno 111
Ellen Anderson 33
Elsie Krug 15, 61, 74-75
Emile Jumeau 82
Emmental, Berne Canton 146-147
Empress Josephine 93
ENGLAND (See *UNITED KINGDOM*) 157
English 20
Eskimo, Native American....................61, 168
ESTONIA 35
Ethel Washington 168
Ets. G. Convert 39
Eugene-Constant Barrois 13, 131

Evzone..........59
Extremadura Region..........137

F

Fainges, Marjory..........11, 112
Faldetta..........120
False Face..........21
Fana..........106
Fearn Brown..........27, 64
Federation Nationale Des Costumes Suisses....146
Fehrle, Anna..........53
Fez..........8, 73, 150
Finistere Department..........43, 46-47
FINLAND..........36-37
Finnic People..........126
Flamenco..........134
Flanders..........14
Flashes..........158
Fleischmann, Margaret E. & Suzanne..........157
Foustanella..........59
FRANCE..........5, 38-48, 50, 93
François Gaultier..........14, 58
French Indo China..........89
Fulani..........64
Funin..........33

G

Gallardete..........111
GAMBIA..........49
Gatya..........67-68
Gaucho..........10, 172
Gaultier, François..........14, 58
Gebrüder Heubach..........174
Gebrüder Kühnlenz..........50
Geisha..........83-84
Geispolsheim..........41
George IV, King..........159
GERMANY..........41, 50-57
Gerzon..........99
Ghoutra..........130
Gjurdin..........8
Glengarry..........159
Gorale..........118
Gorge Du Dades..........97
GREECE..........58-60
GREENLAND..........61
Gregory, Jane & Sarah..........17, 27, 169
Groninger, Margaret..........16, 33
GUATEMALA..........62-63
Gudbandstal..........109
Guerande..........45
GUINEA..........64
Gumbaz..........130
Gutach..........53
Gyantso, Tashi..........25

H

H' Moong (Mong)..........89
Halsmantel..........53
Hamburg..........57
Hamburg State..........57
Hanauer Area..........50

Hardänger Area..........106-107
Hathaway, Mary..........34, 113
Hausa People..........105
Havik Dolls..........101
Hawaii..........170
Heddal..........108
Hei Mana Creations..........170
Helena, Maria..........119
Hesse State..........51
Heubach, Gebrüder..........174
Highland..........159
Hill Tribes Federation..........151
Hluk..........31
HOLLAND (See NETHERLANDS)..........5, 99-103
Holz, Loretta..........71, 153
Hong Kong..........22
Hopi, Native American..........164
Hordaland County..........106-107
Howard, Betsy..........158
Huaraches..........62
Hudson's Bay..........20
Hudson's Bay Company..........20
Huik..........120
Huipil..........62-63, 95
Huipil Chico..........96
Huipil Grande..........96
Hula Kahiko..........170
HUNGARY..........3, 5, 65-68
Husk Face..........21
Hutzul..........118

I

ICELAND..........69
Ichimatsu..........85
Ideal Toy Co...........90
Igaal..........130
Ikat..........86, 173
Ilse Ludecke..........54
INDIA..........70-71
Indo China, French..........89
INDONESIA..........72-73
Ingeborg Nielsen..........5, 33
Ingelstad Harad..........144-145
Inuit..........61
Ionian Islands..........60
IRAN..........74
IRELAND..........75
Iroquois, Native Canadian..........21
Islam..........131
ITALY..........5, 39, 76-80

J

JAMAICA..........81
Janosik..........118
JAPAN..........82-86
Java..........72-73
Jewish..........41
Jizba Krasna..........133
João Perotti Manufactura Orbis..........16
JORDAN..........87
Josephine, Empress..........93
Judean Hills..........87

Jumeau, Emile..........82
Jutland..........33

K

Kabuki..........83
Kabul..........7
Kachina..........164
Kalocsa Region..........65
Kämmer & Reinhardt..........55, 127, 155, 159
Kanaar, Patty & Peggy Hinshaw
     (Hei Mana Creations)..........170
Käthe Kruse..........53, 55
Katherine Dunham..........16
Kenejestewa, LeRoy..........164
KENYA..........88
Kerfeunteun..........43
Kham..........25
Kierpce..........118
Kiev..........155
Kimono..........82-86
Kimport..........5, 8, 10-11, 17-19, 21, 24, 29, 36, 39, 54, 60, 66, 73-75, 89, 92, 98, 111, 113-116, 118-121, 126, 143, 149, 171, 175
King George IV..........159
Kirkkonummi..........36
Klompen..........103
Klumpe..........138-139
Knüsli, Laura..........53, 147
Kolle-Hat..........109
Kopparberg Province..........143
Koran..........105
Koto Missie..........140
Kotula..........29
Kovacs, "Marika"..........3
Krakow..........116, 118
Kraplap..........102
Kristianstadt & Malmohus Provinces..........144-145
Krug, Elsie..........15, 61, 74-75
Krug International Doll House..........15, 33, 149
Kruse, Käthe..........53, 55
Kühnlenz, Gebrüder..........50
Kukeri..........18
Kukinova, Alexandra..........125
Kurzeme Province..........90
Kyjov..........32

L

La Mode..........97
La Montuna..........111
La Pollera..........111
Lagartera..........138
Lake Pátzcuaro District..........95
Lambadi..........70
Lang's..........104
LAOS..........89, 151
Lapa..........56
Lapland..........37, 108
Las Tablas..........111
Latium..........76-77
LATVIA..........90
Lauder, Sir Harry..........158
Lazio Compartimento..........76-77

Le Minor 41, 46-48
Lefkas 60
Lei 170
Lenci 16, 77, 79-80, 135
Lencilandia 16
LeRoy Kenejestewa 164
Les Poupées Cadette 48
Les Poupées Du Venthievre 46
Les Poupées Magali.....................................38-39
Les Poupées Sandra Dogue 93
LESOTHO 91
Lesotho Cooperative Handicrafts 91
Lidova Tvorba...133
Liguria 39
Litham 97
Loire-Atlantique Department 45
London, England..157
Lowicz Commune 117
Ludecke, Ilse 54
Lum, Ada 22
Luneburg 57

Mitsu-Ore Ningyo (Triple-Jointed Dolls)............85
Mittelland 146
Moccasins 164
Mols Peninsula 33
Monaco 39
Moon, Wanda 169
Moravia 30, 31-32
Moravian-Slovak 31
Morbihan Department 43
MORDVIA AUTONOMOUS REPUBLIC 126
More & Romsdal County 109
Moro People 115
MOROCCO 97-98
Mrs. Viji Srinivasan 71
Munsala 36
Muskhogean Indians 167
Muslim 49, 105

Owanyudane Craft Guild 21

P

Pages S.A. (Inc.) 135
PAKISTAN 110
PANAMA 111
PAPUA-NEW GUINEA 112
Pearlies 157
Pedigree...81
Peljesac Peninsula 29
Peloponnesus 59
Perez, Sociedad Anómina, Mariquita 134
Perotti Manufactura Orbis, João 16
Persia (See IRAN) 74
PERU 113
Petitcollin.............................38, 46-47, 93
Petterssen, Ronnaug 5, 108
PHILIPPINES 114-115
Piana Dei Greci..79
Pickering, Barbara 23
Plaide 158-159
Pokamiso 58
POLAND....................................5, 116-118
Poltava 155
Polynesian 170
Pont-Aven 46
Pont l' Abbé 47
PORTUGAL 119-120
Powell, Violet M. 75
Preveza Department 60
Protestants..41, 103
Provence 39
Pueblo Indians...164
Puszta 68

M

MACEDONIA 92
Magis...77
Maharaja 71
Malaby, Miss A.G. 87
Malays 115
Malmohus Province.................................144-145
Mandarin 23
Mandarin Square 23
Maori People 104
Marama 122
Marga (See Margit Szerelemhegyi) 5, 66
Margaret E. & Suzanne Fleischmann 157
Margit Szerelemhegyi 5, 66
Maria Cavanova 32
Maria Helena 119
Maria Veleva 17
Marika 3
Mariova 92
Mariquita Perez Sociedad Anómina 134
Maritime Province 19
Marken 99-100
Marseille, Armand 29, 49, 56, 99, 101, 109, 163
MARTINIQUE 93
Martta (Martha) 36-37
Marwari People..71
Masai People 88
Mate 10
Mattaldi 10
Mehedintzi District 122-123
Meo (Miao) People 89
Metti/Netta 112
MEXICO 94-96
    Post Conquest 94
Mezokovesd 66-67
Michoácan 95
Midgley. Sarah Baron 11
Minho Province...119
Mintan 8
Miranda, Carmen 16, 94
Miss A.G. Malaby...87

N

Nagpada Neighborhood House 71
Najd 130
Naples 78
Napoli 78
Narodna Radinost 5, 175
Native American (See UNITED STATES) 163
    Eastern Woodlands 163
    Hopi 164
    Iñupiat People (Eskimo) 168
    Navajo 165
    Seminole 167
    Shoshoni 169
Native Canadians 20-21
Navajo, Native American 165
Near East Industries 8, 60, 92
Nebaj Village...62
NEPAL 25
NETHERLANDS 5, 99-103
New Brunswick 19
NEW ZEALAND 104
Nica 90
Nice 39
Nielsen, Ingeborg 5, 33
NIGERIA 105
Niste 139
Nodders 23
Noord Holland Province 99-101
Normandy 48
NORWAY 5, 37, 106-109
Novosilyevsky Region 125

O

Obi 82-86
Ocú 111
Odense...33
Old Cottage Toys 157
Oltenia Region......................................122-123
Opanki 28, 174-175
Orebic 29
Orissa State 71
Ost Telemark County 108
Ottoman 8-9
Otztal Valley 13

Q

Quimper Arrondissment 43

R

Ramallah 87
Rajasthan State 71
Ratiskovice 32
Rättvik..5, 143
Ravca, Bernard 149
Rebozo...94-95
Red Jacket Costume 108
Reliable 111
Rheinsche Gummi und Celluloid-Fabrik 143
Rhine River 50
Riga 105
Roldan 139
Roma 5, 76-77
ROMANIA 121-123
Rome 76
Romsdal County 109
Ronnaug Pettersssen.................................5, 108
Rosalie Whyel Museum of Doll Art 4, 7, 15,
....27, 32, 37, 87
Rubac 133
RUSSIA 4, 37, 124-129
Ryazan Region...127-128

S

S.F.B.J. (Société Française de Fabrication de
  Bébés et Jouets) 45, 93
Saaremaa Island 35
Sahara 97
Saille 45
Salamis 58
Samso Island 33
San Cristobal Totonicapan 63
Sarah Baron Midgley 11
Sari 71
SAUDI ARABIA 130
Savarah People 71
Scaer 43
Scapulaires 43
Schildkröte 143
Schlappe 146
Schoenau And Hoffmeister 76
Schwalm 51
Schwarzwald 50, 53-55
Scotland (See *UNITED KINGDOM*) 158-159
Scott, Sir Walter 159
Seminole, Native American 167
SENEGAL 49, 131-132
Serape 94
Serbia (See *YUGOSLAVIA*) 174-175
Sessa Arunca 78
Seville 134
Shanghai 24
Shayla 130
Shkoder (Scutari) 8
Shona 176
Shope 17
Shoshonean 164
Shoshoni, Native American 169
Siberia (See *RUSSIA*) 129
Sicily Compartimento (See *ITALY*) 79
Simon & Halbig 51, 103, 107, 127
Sindh Province 110
Sir Harry Lauder 158
Sir Walter Scott 159
Sirwaal 130
Sjaelland Island Group 33
Skåne Region 144-145
Skaut 106
Skookum Indian 167
SLIP (Slovak Home Industries) 31
Slovak Home Industries (SLIP) 31
SLOVAK REPUBLIC (See *SLOVAKIA*) 31, 133
SLOVAKIA 31, 133
Sobre Pantalones 63
Société Française de Fabrication de Bébés
  et Jouets (S.F.B.J.) 45, 93
Société Nobel Française 38, 41, 93
Sofia 17
Sombrero 94
Sont Nathu 71
Sorbs 56
Soukman 17
SOUTH AFRICA (See *UNION OF
  SOUTH AFRICA*) 156
South Africa Red Cross Society 156
South America 10

Soviet Union (See *RUSSIA*) 125-127, 129
Soviet Union (See *UKRAINE*) 155
SPAIN 134-139
Spakenberg Village 102
Spanish 114
Sporran 158-159
Spreewald District 56
Srinivasan, Mrs. Viji 70
Strandy 33
Strasbourg 41
Struga-Ohrid Area 92
Sulu Province 115
Sumadija Region 174-175
Sunnmore 109
SURINAM 140
Swaine And Company 32
SWAZILAND 141
SWEDEN 5, 37, 142-145
SWITZERLAND 5, 146-148
SYRIA 5, 149-150
Szerelemhegyi, Margit 5, 66
Szur 68

T

Tabi 83, 86
TAJIKISTAN 173
TANZANIA 88
Tarboosh 8, 150
Tartan 158-159
Tashi Gyantso 25
Tatra Mountains 118
Tehuantepec 96
Tembleques 111
THAILAND 151-152
Thawb 130
Thomann, Adolf & Paul (Studio) 147
Tibet (see *CHINA*) 25
Tibeto-Burman 151-152
Tiki 104
Toledo, Spain 138-139
Toorie 158
Totonicapan 63
Tovaglia 76
Trans-Danube 3
Transylvania 121, 123
Trecianska Area 133
TRINIDAD 153
Tropicrafts 34
Tsaroukia 59-60
Tuareg People 97
Tula Province 125
TURKEY 154
TURKMENISTAN 173
Tyrol 13

U

Uchikake 83
Uhersky Brod 31
UKRAINE 155
Ulster Province 75
UNION OF SOUTH AFRICA 156
UNITED KINGDOM 157-160

UNITED STATES 161-171
URUGUAY 10, 172
Uta Brauser 161-162
Utrecht Province 102
Utsang 25
UZBEKISTAN 173

V

Val Gardena Valley 80
Valdres 109
Valencia 135-136
Vana Mustjala 35
Vecchiotti, Alberani 79
Veleva, Maria 17
Velvalee Dickinson 33, 98
Venezia Tridentia Compartimento 80
Viana Do Castelo District 119
Vierlande District 57
Viji Srinivasan 71
Vilnic 122
Violet M. Powell 75
Virgin Islands (See *UNITED STATES*) 171
Virgin Islands Native Products 171
Vlcnov 31
Voit, Andreas 57
Volendam 5, 101
Voss 106-107
Vraka 60

W

Wales (See *UNITED KINGDOM*) 160
Wanda Moon 169
Warszawa Department 117
Washington, Ethel 168
Weibull, Charlotte 144-145
Wends 56
Wenham Museum 23, 63, 126
Whitsuntide 31
Wolof People 49, 131-132
Wright, Barton 164
Württemberg 53-55
Wyoming 169

Y

Yakutia Autonomous Republic 129
Yeshi, Kim 25
YUGOSLAVIA 5, 92, 174-175
Yunnan Province 151

Z

Zagorsk (see *RUSSIA*) 127, 155
Zagreb 28
Zeeland Province 103
ZIMBABWE 176
Zori 86
Zuid-Beveland Area 103
Zulu 156
Zygmunt K. Allina 5, 118